THE
3-INGREDIENT
BAKING BOOK

THE

3-INGREDIENT BAKING BOOK

101 SIMPLE, SWEET & STRESS-FREE RECIPES

Charmian Christie

Library and Archives Canada Cataloguing in Publication
Title: The 3-ingredient baking book : 101 simple, sweet & stress-free recipes / Charmian Christie.
Other titles: Three-ingredient baking book
Names: Christie, Charmian, author.
Description: Includes index.
Identifiers: Canadiana 20190107596 | ISBN 9780778806349 (softcover)
Subjects: LCSH: Baking. | LCGFT: Cookbooks.
Classification: LCC TX763 .C47 2019 | DDC 641.81/5—dc23

Disclaimer
The recipes in this book have been carefully tested by our kitchen and our tasters. To the best of our knowledge, they are safe and nutritious for ordinary use and users. For those people with food or other allergies, or who have special food requirements or health issues, please read the suggested contents of each recipe carefully and determine whether or not they may create a problem for you. All recipes are used at the risk of the consumer.

We cannot be responsible for any hazards, loss or damage that may occur as a result of any recipe use.

For those with special needs, allergies, requirements or health problems, in the event of any doubt, please contact your medical adviser prior to the use of any recipe.

Cover and book design: Kevin Cockburn/PageWave Graphics Inc.
Cover and interior photography: Lauren Miller
Editors: Meredith Dees and Sue Sumeraj
Copyeditor, Proofreader & Indexer: Gillian Watts
Recipe Editor: Jennifer MacKenzie
Food Styling: Dara Sutin
Prop Styling: Rayna Schwartz

The publisher gratefully acknowledges the financial support of our publishing program by the Government of Canada through the Canada Book Fund.

Canadä

Published by Robert Rose Inc.
120 Eglinton Avenue East, Suite 800, Toronto, Ontario, Canada M4P 1E2
Tel: (416) 322-6552 Fax: (416) 322-6936
www.robertrose.ca

Printed and bound in Canada

1 2 3 4 5 6 7 8 9 TCP 27 26 25 24 23 22 21 20 19

To my sisters,
Robin and Allison.

Thank you for your patience,
eager taste-testing,
honest feedback, encouragement,
support, and most of all
help with the endless
sink-loads of dishes.

You both get double portions
of everything
for life.

CONTENTS

Three ingredients?

Really?

Yes, really.

INTRODUCTION

Those who know me will vouch that I'm no minimalist. I can complicate anything. *Anything.* Ask me to slice a few strawberries and, half a pint into the process, I'll be plotting out a Rum-Soaked–Strawberry-Balsamic-Pistachio Jam. Questioning what to do with chocolate? I'll suggest a Mocha-Hazelnut-Orange Dacquoise. Ice cream? What starts with Whisky-Kissed Brown Sugar and ends with Buttered-Pecan Bits? You'd think I'd run out of hyphens.

So, what's an over-the-top, hyphen-loving flavor-stacker like me doing writing a three-ingredient cookbook? Well, there is one hyphen, so I'm in familiar territory. There are also requests from non-baking friends and family, as well as clients who take my classes. They all want simple recipes they can make with items they have on hand or can get with a single trip to just one grocery store. They don't want a list of ingredients longer than their Visa bill or that requires a trek to three specialty shops. They want easy, uncomplicated recipes that deliver delicious results.

I'll admit, I began this book to accommodate them and get some peace. But as I worked with the limited ingredient lists, I began to see that more isn't always better. There is joy in a simple peanut butter cookie, and mango sorbet doesn't need much help. This revelation built momentum, and soon I found I'd rolled past straight-up baking and careened headfirst into other sweets — like ice cream, mousse, chocolates and sauces.

If you're new to baking, this book is a good place to start. Nothing here is too difficult, and you won't have to spend a car payment on specialized pans. If you're a seasoned cook, I hope you'll find inspiration and a few new ways to make old favorites without the fuss.

Regardless of your experience level, grab an apron, set out some bowls and bake with abandon!

— CHARMIAN

MUST-HAVE EQUIPMENT

It's easy to get carried away with kitchen gadgets. Pricey copper bowls, adorable cat-shaped measuring spoons, and quirky egg separators tug at our purse strings. I want you to save your money — and your kitchen space. Here is what you need to bake successfully from this book.

BAKING PANS

Need and *want* are two different things. I *want* that fancy four-turret Bundt pan shaped like a fairy castle. I *need* a run-of-the-mill muffin pan. While stores are full of decorative options, those expensive one-trick-pony pans rarely earn their keep. The recipes in this book call for standard pans that can be found in the kitchen section of almost any grocery store or department store (or online). Buy what you need as you go. You can bake your way through this entire book using the following pans:

Baking sheets (2): Sizes vary wildly. If you have baking sheets, use what you have. If you don't, then get the biggest that can fit in your oven. When buying new pans, keep in mind that dark baking sheets can brown items too quickly, while thin sheets tend to warp and just don't deliver even heat. Look for heavy sheets with a light color. If you already own thin baking sheets and find that your cookies burn, double up the pans. Nonstick sheets damage easily. Avoid them if you can. They aren't necessary if you have parchment paper or a silicone baking mat on hand.

I always buy rimmed sheets for their versatility. They can bake cookies as well as be used for items that could spill, such as Sponge Toffee (page 174), Tuxedo Chocolate Bark (page 115) and Balsamic Roasted Strawberries (page 136). If a recipe needs a rimmed pan, it will be specified in the equipment list.

Glass baking dish (13 by 9 inches/33 by 23 cm): This dish is versatile. You can use it to bake a big batch of squares or to chill Peach Sherbet (page 188). It's also equivalent to two 8-inch (20 cm) square dishes, so

you can double a Black Forest Fudge recipe (page 170) or make an extra-big batch of Chocolate Almond Crunchies (page 56) without worrying about overfilling the dish. (And yes, overfilling is an issue. See page 23 for details.)

Loaf pan (9 by 5 inches/23 by 12.5 cm): A small loaf pan proves invaluable when chilling frozen treats such as Strawberry Ice Cream (page 191) and Mango Sorbet (page 192).

Mini-muffin pan (24 cups): This is useful for unbaked chocolate desserts, creating perfect bite-sized treats — think Chocolate Peanut Butter Cups (page 112) and Chocolate-Filled Raspberries (page 120). Since I rarely use it for baked goods, I bought a heavy pan with a nonstick coating so any drips that escape the liners can be cleaned up easily. If you plan on using the pan for traditional baking, get a heavy, light-colored one that isn't nonstick, and stock up on liners.

Muffin pans (12 cups): Of course, you can make muffins in these — Raspberry Ice-Cream Muffins (page 85) and Mandarin Muffins (page 86) spring to mind — but they work just as well for tarts, mini-cheesecakes and other treats. Buy a pan (or two, if you're ambitious) that's light in color but heavy in weight, for even cooking. They stack neatly for storing, so a second pan won't take up much more room, and having two is handy if you decide to make more than 12 treats.

Round cake pan (8 inches/20 cm): Round pans are the classic shape for cakes, be they chocolate or cheese. Get a heavy, light-colored round pan and you'll be ready for the next birthday. (Mine is in June. Just sayin'.)

Square baking dishes and pans (8 inches/ 20 cm, glass and metal): I use glass dishes for fruit cobblers and recipes that call for acids like lemon juice. Acidic food made in a reactive metal pan, such as aluminum or cast iron, can taste metallic and get stained. For almost everything else, I use metal pans. They are more lightweight than glass, don't break, and stack more easily. Not sure which to use? Don't worry — I specify in the recipe if it matters.

BEYOND PANS

Kitchen scale: This gadget scares a lot of people. I get it — it takes the art out of baking and turns it into a science project. Will I change your mind if I tell you a scale makes measuring much faster, reduces cleanup times and improves accuracy? All the recipes in this book include ingredient weights, where practical. For very little money, kitchen scales can be purchased in grocery stores and department stores. Digital scales are easy to use and can be set to provide either metric or imperial options. Why not give it a go?

Ice-pop molds: Most ice-pop molds come in 1/3 cup (75 mL) and 1/2 cup (125 mL) sizes. While mold size won't affect the finished product, it will influence your yield and can extend freezing time. This is why the ice-pop recipes in this book give a range (for example, 6 to 9 ice pops) rather than an exact count. When it comes to shapes, you can buy whimsical rockets or stars, but traditional paddle molds work well for any recipe. If you don't have ice-pop molds, use paper Dixie cups and insert a wooden stick when the filling is semi-frozen.

No matter which mold you use, filling them can be a sloppy job. Reduce spills by transferring the ice-pop mixture to a spouted measuring cup before pouring, or use a spouted ladle.

Measuring cups (dry ingredients): These scoops are designed to measure ingredients that don't pour, such as flour, sugar, dried fruit, nuts and oats. Get a set that has as many sizes as possible. Mine has scoops that measure 1/4 cup (60 mL), 1/3 cup (75 mL), 1/2 cup (125 mL), 2/3 cup (150 mL), 3/4 cup (175 mL) and 1 cup (250 mL). I use them all!

Measuring cups (wet ingredients): Designed to measure anything liquid, such as water, juice, cream, milk and wine (for cooking, not for the cook), this cup's distinctive spout and handle make pouring a breeze. I prefer glass to plastic, since I often deal with hot liquids. I use my tiny 1/4-cup (60 mL) measure a lot, especially for lemon juice, but most people will find they need only a 1-cup (250 mL) and a 2-cup (500 mL) measure.

Measuring spoons: One set is essential. Two will buy you peace of mind. Having stuck a damp teaspoon into the baking soda more than once, I now have separate sets of measuring spoons: one for wet ingredients like vanilla and honey, the other for dry. My sets have slim bowls and long handles; they are slender enough to fit into narrow spice jars and long enough to scrape the bottom. Get a set with as many sizes as possible, from 1/8 teaspoon (0.5 mL) all the way through to 1 tablespoon (15 mL).

Microplane-style zester: This is my go-to utensil for many things. I use it for zesting citrus but also for grating a wide range of ingredients, including chocolate, nutmeg, cinnamon stick, gingerroot, garlic (bye-bye, garlic press!) and Parmesan cheese.

Mixing bowls (glass or stainless steel): Glass and stainless steel bowls are best, since they chill well for whipping cream and don't react with mixtures that have a lot of acid in them, such as Ginger-Crusted Lime Tarts (page 161). Plastic bowls are lightweight and kid-friendly, but they have limits. They can absorb odors, cause issues when whipping egg whites (see page 23) and might not be microwave-safe. If possible, get a nesting set that contains a small, a medium and a large bowl. Some recipes call for two bowls, so second medium and large bowls will also come in handy.

Paper liners for muffins: A standard 12-cup muffin pan takes large liners. But not all liners are created equal. Parchment liners will not stick to your baked goods, but they're on the pricey side. Fancy foil liners come with decorative patterns on the outside and shiny foil on the inside; they're wonderful for special occasions and work well, but they are even more expensive than their parchment counterparts. Paper liners are inexpensive but often tear your muffins when removed. To avoid this, place paper liners in the pan and give them a quick spritz of cooking spray or a light brushing with cooking oil before filling. Problem solved.

If you have mini-muffin pans, look for mini-muffin or truffle-cup liners. They come in parchment, foil and paper, just like their bigger cousins.

Parchment paper: This culinary paper is not to be confused with waxed paper. Unlike waxed paper, whose coating can melt at low temperatures, parchment paper is coated with a thin layer of silicone and can withstand temperatures up to 450°F (230°C). Parchment paper prevents food from sticking to the pan, makes cleanup easier, can be used as a divider when stacking baked goods for storage, and is generally my must-have item of choice. I also find it more versatile than reusable silicone baking mats, which don't always fit my baking sheet.

When it comes to fitting into corners or round pans, parchment can be a bit uncooperative. Fortunately, you can wrestle it into submission. Just turn on the kitchen faucet and crumple the parchment into a ball under gently running water. It will become limp like a wet dishcloth. Unfold the wadded parchment, shake off the excess water and then press it into your pan and pat dry with a clean towel. It will look a bit rumpled but it will stay in place. Leave a few inches hanging over the edge of the pan; the extra can be used as handles for easy removal later.

Rolling pin: Rolling pins are not just for pastry anymore! I use mine to break up Mixed

Nut Brittle (page 179), crush gingersnaps, and threaten people who try to sneak cookies. Use whatever type of pin you like, be it wooden or silicone, straight or tapered. No pin? Grab a wine bottle and get rolling.

Spatulas (1 large and 1 mini): Spatulas are my go-to utensil, right after the Microplane. If you don't have any, be sure to buy ones that are made of heat-resistant silicone. If you can buy a preassembled set of spatulas in varying sizes, you'll be set. Otherwise, get two — one tiny spatula for scraping out tins of condensed milk, and one large, curved spatula (sometimes called a spoonula), which can scrape clean big bowls and double as a mixing spoon.

Whisk: This tool is handier than you think. Unless you plan on whisking eggs and cream by hand, you don't need a gigantic balloon whisk. Instead, invest in a medium-sized whisk about 10 to 12 inches (25 to 30 cm) long. It's ideal for blending dry ingredients and stirring pots of liquid on the stove. A small whisk (about the size of a teaspoon) isn't essential but comes in handy if you make a lot of mug cakes.

Wire cooling racks (2): As their name indicates, cooling racks allow baked goods to cool, but they are also handy for creating drizzled treats such as Pretzel Snaps (page 173). Just place something under the rack to catch the drips. Wire racks are handy and stack easily, so buy two.

DAIRY

Butter: The recipes in this book call for salted butter. Grocery store butter is fine, but if a high-end brand goes on sale, stock up. Once you get home, wrap the packaged butter in plastic, put it in a resealable freezer bag and freeze for up to 6 months. Defrost frozen butter in the refrigerator overnight. For baking, most recipes require room-temperature butter. See page 24 for a quick way to bring butter to room temperature without melting it.

Dulce de leche: This is caramelized sweetened condensed milk. It's like a thick caramel sauce that can be used to sweeten Caramel Apple Tarts (page 107), drizzled over Vanilla Ice Cream (page 184) or used as the base of a classic Portuguese mousse called Baba de Camelo (page 152). You can find it in most grocery stores with the sauces and syrups or in the Latin foods section.

Heavy or whipping (35%) cream: This cream has about 35% butter fat and is often used in ganache or to make whipped cream. The secret to good whipped cream is simple — keep the cream refrigerated until the last minute.

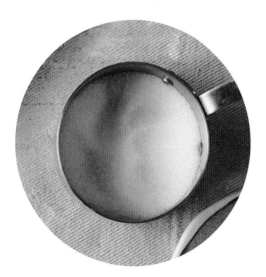

Sweetened condensed milk: Thick as honey, this tasty combination of sugar and milk is often used to sweeten and bind no-bake treats and ice cream. Because it's been boiled down, there is very little water to evaporate. Don't confuse this with evaporated milk, which is not sweetened and is quite liquid. The recipes in this book call for full-fat sweetened condensed milk. Substituting a lower-fat or non-fat milk could lead to disappointment.

SUGARS

Brown sugar: This sugar contains varying degrees of molasses and imparts caramel and butterscotch notes. Unless the recipe specifies amber or light brown sugar, for me the darker the better, but that's just a matter of taste. While demerara is my favorite, brown sugar of any kind will work in these recipes. But be warned — unlike granulated sugar, brown sugar can dry out quickly. Keep it in an airtight bag with the air squeezed out. If the sugar hardens, heat it in a microwave-safe bowl in the microwave on High in 30-second intervals, stirring in between, until softened. To measure packed brown sugar, spoon it into a dry measure and press down to compact it enough; when the sugar is turned out of the measure, it should hold its shape.

Confectioners' (icing) sugar: Also called powdered sugar, this sweetener contains sugar and cornstarch. The cornstarch adds stability, while the ultra-fine sugar dissolves quickly. If it's lumpy, sift it through a fine-mesh sieve before measuring. This sugar is invaluable in Chantilly Cream (page 206), Chocolate Chip Icebox Cake (page 76) and Chocolate Mug Cake (page 80).

Granulated sugar: Also known as white sugar or table sugar, this is the most common sugar in the store. Stored in an airtight container in a cool, dry pantry, it will keep indefinitely.

OTHER INGREDIENTS

Chocolate: Good-quality chocolate can be found right in your grocery store — all you have to do is read the label. Avoid compound chocolate or anything labeled "chocolatey." Real chocolate contains cocoa butter. Quality dark chocolate will list cocoa beans (sometimes called cocoa mass) first, while white and milk chocolate will have cocoa butter as the second ingredient after sugar. Regardless of the type of chocolate you're buying, if it's made with modified oils, modified milk products, vanillin (not a typo!) or artificial flavors, put the bar back on the shelf and keep looking. Chances are that a good-quality option is within arm's reach. Most of the chocolate in this book is dark, and I use 70 percent dark chocolate.

White chocolate: A couple of the recipes in this book call for caramelizing white chocolate. When making your own caramelized white chocolate, use good-quality white chocolate with a high percentage of cocoa butter — at least 30%. This process will not work with white chocolate chips or low-quality white chocolate.

Caramelizing white chocolate takes time, but the end result keeps as long as regular white chocolate, about 4 months. Make a double batch in a 13- by 9-inch (33 by 23 cm) glass baking dish so you'll have lots on hand the next time you crave caramelized white chocolate (which you probably will). Pour it into an airtight container and leave uncovered until cooled to room temperature. Cover and store in a cool, dark place.

Chocolate chips: Tasty as they may be, chocolate chips are not the same as chocolate. They are designed to keep their shape when heated, unlike regular chocolate, which will dissolve into a puddle. Chips cannot be used in place of chocolate unless the recipe says so. However, if a recipe in this book calls for chocolate chips, the semisweet, milk and white chocolate varieties can be used interchangeably.

MELTING CHOCOLATE

Most recipes in this book call for melting chocolate in the microwave. You'll notice that the times vary with the kind of chocolate used. White chocolate melts faster and scorches more easily, so it often has a shorter heating time. If you don't have a microwave or your microwave tends to heat unevenly, chocolate can be melted on the stovetop — it just takes a bit more attention. This method works with all kinds of chocolate, including chocolate chips.

To ensure that your chocolate melts smoothly and doesn't burn:

1 Chop the chocolate into small pieces about the size of chocolate chips.

2 Place the chocolate in a heatproof bowl over 1 inch (2.5 cm) of simmering (not boiling) water, making sure the bottom of the bowl doesn't touch the water. (If the recipe specifies, other ingredients such as cream, milk or butter can be added at the same time as the chocolate.)

3 As the chocolate melts, give it a gentle stir now and again. Adjust the heat as necessary to prevent the water from steaming — if steam gets into the bowl, the chocolate may seize, becoming granular and lumpy. When the chocolate is almost fully melted, remove it from the heat and stir gently to dissolve the remaining bits. The timing will depend on the amount of chocolate, the size of the bowl and the temperature of the water. (Go extra slowly with white chocolate, as it scorches more easily than dark; you can even remove the pan from the heat to avoid the water getting too hot.)

Citrus: Lemon, lime, orange and even grapefruit zest (a.k.a. peel) adds color, fragrance and life to recipes. When zesting citrus, the secret is to take off only the colorful outer layer and leave the bitter white pith on the fruit. Once citrus has been zested, the fruit dries out quickly if left in the open and it goes moldy if wrapped. So what do you do? Whenever a recipe calls for either freshly squeezed juice or grated zest, prepare both and freeze what you don't need (see below).

FREEZING ZEST

Grate the fruit with a Microplane-style zester (page 12) or the small holes of a box grater. Place any unused zest in a small airtight container and store in the freezer. It will keep for up to 1 year. Whenever a recipe calls for zest, you'll have a stash on hand. There's no need to defrost frozen zest. Be sure to label the container with the date to avoid UFOs (Unidentified Frozen Objects) — frozen lemon and orange zest look almost alike.

FREEZING JUICE

Before the freshly grated fruit has a chance to go bad, juice it and remove any seeds. You will get more juice out of your citrus if you zap it in the microwave on High for 10 to 15 seconds and then roll it on the counter, pressing firmly with your palms. (Do this before you zest the fruit, or you could end up with juice all over your counter.)

Fresh juice can be refrigerated for 2 to 3 days, but for longer storage, pour it into the compartments of an ice-cube tray — each will hold about 1 tablespoon (15 mL) juice. Freeze and then transfer the frozen juice cubes to a resealable plastic bag or an airtight container; store in the freezer for quick retrieval. Frozen lemon juice will keep for up to 1 year, but its flavor will begin to degrade after 6 months. Be sure to label the bag; once frozen, lemon and lime juice look remarkably similar.

Cocoa powder (unsweetened): Made from dried, defatted cocoa beans, cocoa powder delivers a lot of flavor and richness but contains no actual cocoa butter. All supermarkets stock cocoa. The recipes in this book can use either natural or Dutch-processed cocoa. One note of caution: don't confuse unsweetened cocoa powder with instant cocoa, which is a sugar-loaded hot chocolate mix.

Eggs: Brown or white, free-range or cage-free, organic or omega-3 — it doesn't matter. Just make sure you use large eggs that are free from cracks. On page 17 are some tips on how to get the most out of whatever eggs you choose to buy.

Oats (quick-cooking rolled): Oats present a bit of a Goldilocks scenario. For the oat-based recipes in this book, steel-cut oats would be far too hard, while instant oatmeal would be far too soft. But quick-cooking rolled oats? They're just right. If you don't have quick-cooking oats on hand, use large-flake (old-fashioned) rolled oats pulsed in a food processor or blender until roughly chopped.

Puff pastry: Commercial puff pastry is a handy alternative to homemade. But be warned: not all commercial pastry is created equal. Look for a brand made with real butter rather than modified oils or margarine.

Puff pastry can be a bit tricky in terms of timing. For best results, defrost the pastry overnight in the refrigerator. In a pinch, defrost it on the counter at room temperature, but keep an eye on it, since you need to roll it while it's still cold. Regardless of how you defrost the pastry, make sure it's soft enough to unroll

NO-FAIL EGG SEPARATING

Eggs separate best when cold, but the whites whip up best when at room temperature. However, even a tiny bit of shell or yolk will prevent the whites from whipping. Don't tempt fate by separating all your egg whites into the same bowl. Chances are the last egg you crack will break its yolk and contaminate all your carefully separated whites. To avoid disaster, crack one egg at a time and release the contents into a small bowl. With clean hands, scoop out the yolk with your fingers, letting the white fall through into the bowl. Make sure the white is free of eggshell and yolk before placing it with the other whites in a large bowl for beating. Place the yolk in a third bowl. Repeat with each egg. If a tiny chip of shell turns up in the whites, scoop it out with a bigger piece of eggshell.

BEATING EGG WHITES

Whipped egg whites add texture and volume to recipes such as Meringues (page 46), Citrus Almond Cake (page 68) and Baba de Camelo (page 152). Use a larger bowl than you think you'll need, and make sure it's grease-free. Whip room-temperature whites until they reach the stiffness called for in the recipe (see page 23 for troubleshooting egg whites that won't whip). Start with medium speed and increase it to high once the whites get frothy. To test if the egg whites are beaten enough, hold the beater upright. For soft peaks, the whites will stand up but the tips will flop to one side, like an upside-down comma. For stiff peaks, the whites will stand up straight and look shiny.

FREEZING EGGS

There's no reason to waste eggs when a recipe calls for orphaning whites or yolks. The whites freeze beautifully and, once defrosted, can be used in almost any recipe that calls for egg whites. Put them in an airtight freezer-safe container, mark the date and the number of whites and freeze. Use them for recipes such as Italian Almond Cookies (page 33) or Meringues (page 46). Frozen whites will keep for up to 6 months. To defrost, thaw in the refrigerator overnight.

Yolks, on the other hand, don't freeze well. However, you can keep them in the refrigerator for up to 2 days. Just place them in an airtight container and add enough water to cover the yolks (to keep them from drying out), then put the lid on the container and pop them into the fridge. Carefully drain off the water and use them in Crème Brûlée (page 158) or make an extra-rich omelet.

without breaking but still cold to the touch. If the fat in the pastry gets too soft, it will not roll properly. Be sure to dust your work surface and rolling pin with flour before rolling. Follow these simple tricks and you'll be making pastry that looks like it came from a bakery.

Freebies: Every recipe in this book uses three ingredients that are essential to its success. Some, like Simple Shortbread (page 34), have three ingredients from start to finish. Others, such as Spiced Dairy-Free Chocolate Mousse (page 121), have three ingredients plus water. Is that cheating? Am I gaming the system? I don't think so. To hold the ingredient list to three, I consider water, a pinch of salt, and flour for dusting the work surface as "freebies," since they are likely already in your kitchen and are used in tiny quantities and/ or as a recipe aid. That's it. Three-ingredient baking, three free ingredients. Coincidence? I think not.

———

Most baking calls for three ingredients — butter, flour and sugar — before you even get to the flavor enhancers like chocolate chips, raisins and vanilla. As a result, many three-ingredient recipes can be a bit flat or one-note. The following mixtures are easy ways to ramp up some of the simple recipes in this book without eating up vast expanses of cupboard space or hours of your time.

MAKES 4 CUPS (600 G)

This magical mixture of flour, baking powder and salt makes many three-ingredient recipes possible. While you can buy self-rising flour (also called self-raising) in grocery stores or bulk bins, making it yourself takes little time and ensures a fresh supply. Most recipes for homemade self-rising flour make only a single cup (150 g), which defeats the purpose of quick three-ingredient baking. This version, however, produces a more respectable amount without taking up too much cupboard space. Scale up or down as needed.

SELF-RISING FLOUR

4 cups (560 g)
all-purpose flour

•

2 tablespoons (20 g)
baking powder

•

2 teaspoons (10 mL)
salt (see Tips)

1 In a large bowl, whisk together the flour, baking powder and salt until well combined. You cannot overmix at this stage, so err on the side of caution and mix for 30 seconds longer than you think is needed.

2 Use immediately or transfer to an airtight container and store at room temperature for up to 1 year.

TIPS

Unlike table salt, fine sea salt doesn't contain anti-caking agents. You can use table salt, but some people find it has a harsher taste. My preference for this recipe is fine sea salt, which is readily available in the spice section of grocery stores.

If you don't bake often, store the flour mixture in the freezer or refrigerator to extend its shelf life to up to 2 years.

Cinnamon toast was my mother's cure-all. When we were under the weather and refusing to eat, she'd toast some bread, slather it with butter and sprinkle cinnamon sugar on top. She knew we were on the mend when we had the energy to smash the sugar into the toast with the back of a knife. Today I no longer keep cinnamon sugar on hand for medicinal purposes. Instead, I use it to spruce up all kinds of treats, from Cinnamon Roly-Polies (page 37) to Flaming Pineapple (page 135). It also makes a lovely addition to coffee.

CINNAMON SUGAR

1 cup (220 g) granulated sugar

•

¼ cup (25 g) ground cinnamon

•

1 teaspoon (5 mL) ground nutmeg

1 In a medium bowl, combine the sugar, cinnamon and nutmeg.

2 Use immediately or transfer to an airtight container and store at room temperature for up to 6 months. Before using, stir well or shake the container vigorously to ensure even distribution of the spices.

TIPS

This recipe can be doubled, tripled or even quadrupled.

Gingerbread Sugar: Use pumpkin pie spice instead of cinnamon and ground ginger in place of the nutmeg.

Citrus is my go-to fix for bland recipes. I haven't met a dish yet that can't be perked up with a bit of orange zest or a splash of lemon. This citrus sugar can brighten almost any sweet, from Eccles Cakes (page 106) to Italian Almond Cookies (page 33). It also adds life to hot beverages such as tea, coffee and mulled cider.

CITRUS SUGAR

1 tablespoon (15 mL)
grated lemon zest

•

1 tablespoon (15 mL)
grated orange zest

•

1 cup (220 g)
granulated sugar

PREHEAT THE OVEN TO THE LOWEST SETTING, 150°F TO 170°F (70°C TO 80°C)

BAKING SHEET, LINED WITH PARCHMENT PAPER

1 Spread the lemon zest and orange zest in a thin layer on the prepared baking sheet. Bake in the preheated oven until the zest is fragrant and slightly dry, about 10 minutes.

2 Let the zest cool to room temperature on the pan set on a wire rack.

3 In a medium bowl, combine the dried zest and sugar.

4 Use immediately or transfer to an airtight container and store at room temperature for up to 3 months. Before using, stir well or shake the container vigorously to ensure even distribution of the zest throughout the sugar.

TIPS

This recipe can be doubled, tripled or even quadrupled.

Try mixing up the zest to make new flavor combinations. Replace the orange zest with lime zest to make Lemon-Lime Sugar, or replace the lemon zest with grapefruit zest for an Orange-Grapefruit variation.

I started making vanilla sugar because I couldn't bear to throw out vanilla pods once the seeds had been scraped out. The more I made, the more I used it. Give it a try — you'll find that it adds a lovely hint of vanilla to desserts such as Crème Brûlée (page 158) and Peach Sherbet (page 188). Of course, your cup of tea or mug of coffee will appreciate some too.

VANILLA SUGAR

*1 vanilla bean
(whole or the pod with
the seeds scraped out;
see Tips), cut into
2-inch (5 cm) pieces*

•

*2 cups (440 g)
granulated sugar*

•

Pinch sea salt

BLENDER

1 In a blender, combine the vanilla bean pieces, sugar and salt; pulse until a slightly beige powder forms.

2 Use immediately or transfer to an airtight container and store at room temperature for up to 1 year.

TIPS

To scrape the seeds from a vanilla pod, cut the pod in half lengthwise, using the tip of a paring knife. Pry the pod open and scrape the knife blade down the inside of one half. The knife will pick up all the tiny black seeds (called "caviar"). Repeat with the second half of the pod. The seeds can be used in one recipe and the leftover pods can be recycled into vanilla sugar. No wastage!

Sometimes moisture from the vanilla bean can cause the sugar to clump. If it does, grate the lumps on the smallest holes of a box grater to break them apart before using the sugar.

WHAT WENT WRONG?

I get asked this a lot. Sometimes I witness the mistake firsthand during one of my cooking classes. Sometimes a frustrated would-be baker pulls me aside after class and asks me a lot of questions. This section covers the most common reasons why good recipes go bad. If you're suffering from paralyzing culinary frustration, read on for some potential relief.

Do I really have to read the recipe all the way through before starting?

I'm guilty of skipping this step myself on occasion. I sometimes glance at the ingredient list and assume I know where things are going, only to find that a filling needs 4 hours to chill or a sauce has to cool. Read the instructions to see if you have enough time, the right equipment, the space, etc. to make the recipe as intended. If not, don't despair. There's likely another tempting recipe just a few pages away.

Can I substitute ingredients?

Not all ingredients are created equal. For example, chocolate chips don't melt like bittersweet (dark) chocolate. In three-ingredient recipes, there's little wiggle room. While these recipes aren't hard to make, the margin for error is narrow, so avoid substituting. If an alternative will work, I've indicated that in the recipe or the tips.

How important are wet and dry measures?

Very. Wet and dry measures are not the same. Swapping one for another can result in up to 26 percent inaccuracy. (See page 12 for details.)

What if I don't have the right pan or baking sheet size?

Some baked goods need room for air to circulate between the pieces. Some need room to spread or rise. It might be tempting to cram a few extra cookies onto a baking sheet, but often it's better to take the time to bake a second pan (I've indicated this for you in the recipes). Forcing batter for a big cake into a little pan will cause it to sink, undercook, overflow, or all three. The right-sized pan is key to a successful bake and a clean, batter-free oven. Ask me how I know!

Is preheating the oven important?

You bet. Turn on the oven before you assemble the ingredients, pull out pans and search for the measuring spoons. You want it to be on for as long as practical before opening that door. When your oven indicates that it's ready to go, the air inside might be the desired temperature, but the walls aren't. This means the temperature will drop drastically the second you open the door. Once your oven tells you it's reached temperature, wait another 20 minutes (30 is better) before baking, if possible. It could make the difference between culinary success and failure.

Why do your recipes specify room temperature for eggs? Can I use them straight from the refrigerator?

The bad news: cold eggs can affect the texture of baked goods. The good news: you can take eggs from refrigerated to room temperature in less than 2 minutes. Just fill a bowl with hot water (think hot-tub warm, not scalding) and submerge whole, in-the-shell eggs for 1 to 2 minutes. If you separated the eggs while they were still cold (see page 17), you can warm the whites quickly by placing the bowl of whites in a larger bowl of warm water and letting it stand for 5 to 10 minutes. (Alternatively, let the whites stand, covered, at room temperature for 30 minutes before beating.)

Why won't my egg whites whip?

If you pinky-swear you got no shell or yolk in the mix (see page 17) but your egg whites refuse to whip into a meringue, there could be less obvious reasons. Plastic bowls can hold on to grease, so next time use glass or stainless steel. Or if your bowls or beater(s) live on the counter, they could have accumulated residual grease from everyday cooking and frying. Wash and thoroughly dry the bowl and beaters before whipping. Excessive humidity can also prevent egg whites from reaching full volume.

Can I soften butter in the microwave?

Don't tell me — you needed soft butter but didn't have time to let it sit 30 to 45 minutes, so you nuked it and now you have cold butter with a molten center. Been there, done that, found a better way. Skip the microwave and grab the box grater. Using the side with large holes, grate the butter onto a plate or right into the mixing bowl. In 2 minutes it will have softened beautifully and evenly.

Why is my batter so dry/stiff?

Chances are there was a fair amount of liquid left in the mixing bowl or container. Grab a spatula and get scraping. Up to ¼ cup (60 mL) of liquid can be left clinging to the inside of a bowl if you simply pour but don't scrape. This can change the texture and taste of the final product. Scraping is especially important when dealing with thick liquids like condensed milk, honey and cream. Using the correct-sized spatula (see page 13) helps, so grab a big spatula for big bowls and a small one for that can of condensed milk.

Why won't my cream whip?

Whipped cream likes the cold. If your kitchen is really hot and you're having trouble whipping cream, chill the bowl and beaters in the freezer for 10 minutes before whipping. This has saved me more than once during a heatwave.

Why are my cakes/cookies/muffins/scones dry and tough?

Did you use the right measuring tools? (See page 12.) If you did, kudos — you're part of the way there. However, the amount won't be accurate if your flour got compacted by enthusiastic scooping or packing, which can throw a measurement off by 30 percent. Spoon the flour into the dry measuring cup until it's heaping, then level it off with a knife. And don't give up. If you still find that recipes consistently don't work, try using a kitchen scale (see page 12) to measure your ingredients by weight rather than volume. That might be the cure.

Why do my cookies always burn?

If you burn cookies every time you bake, the chances are it's not you — it's the baking sheets. If you don't have time to head to the store for new ones (see page 11 for tips), double up. Once they're stacked one on top of the other, cheap baking sheets make an instant substitute for an expensive insulated pan. Alternatively, try a silicone baking mat. And once your baking is done, buy better pans.

If only some of your cookies are burning, even when you've doubled up the baking sheets or used a silicone baking mat, hot spots in your oven could be to blame. To compensate, rotate the baking sheet midway through cooking. (Note: This works with cookies and muffins, but do not try it with a cake. The cake will likely fall.) For best results, bake one pan at a time on the middle rack of the oven.

I'm dying to see how things are going. Can I peek at my baking?

Curiosity killed the cat — and the cake. Most baked goods don't like to be disturbed. It's tempting to open the door to see how things are going, but unless you need to rotate pans, let the oven timer do its job. Turn on the oven light and look through the window in the door (if it's too dirty to see through, that's another issue).

So, that's about it. What are you waiting for? Grab three ingredients and bake!

COOKIES

Being forgetful has its advantages. One day I baked these right after a batch of Simple Shortbread (page 34) and forgot to raise the oven temperature. Turns out I prefer these cookies baked lower and longer, so my inattention worked in my favor. Wish the laundry worked that way!

PEANUT BUTTER COOKIES

*1 large egg,
at room temperature*

•

*1 cup (260 g)
peanut butter (see Tips)*

•

*1 cup (220 g)
granulated sugar, plus
2 tablespoons (30 mL)
for rolling*

PREHEAT THE OVEN TO 300°F (150°C)

2 BAKING SHEETS, LINED WITH PARCHMENT PAPER

1 In a medium bowl, whisk the egg with a fork. Add the peanut butter and sugar, mixing until smooth.

2 Roll 1 tablespoon (15 mL) dough into a ball. Place 2 tablespoons (30 mL) sugar in a small bowl. Dip one side of the ball in the sugar and place with the sugared side up on the prepared baking sheet. Repeat with the remaining dough, spacing the balls 2 inches (5 cm) apart. Using the tines of a fork to make a crisscross pattern, flatten each cookie to ½ inch (1 cm) thick.

3 Bake, one sheet at a time, on the middle rack of the preheated oven until the edges are set, about 20 minutes.

4 Let cool on the baking sheet for 5 minutes before transferring the cookies to a wire rack to cool completely.

TIPS

This recipe works best with regular sweetened peanut butter, not the unsweetened all-natural variety.

Store the cookies in an airtight container at room temperature for up to 1 week.

These aren't your standard molasses-based cookies spiced with a blend of cinnamon, cloves and ground ginger. These are full-on, no-doubt-about-it, nothing-but-ginger ginger cookies. They are designed to appeal to those of us who consider ourselves Serious Ginger Lovers and can take the heat. Instead of ground ginger, this recipe relies on plenty of crystalized ginger to deliver its signature zing.

GINGER COOKIES

½ cup (75 g)
chopped crystalized
ginger, plus
30 ⅛-inch (3 mm) cubes
for garnish (see Tips)

•

1 cup (140 g)
all-purpose flour

•

½ cup (115 g)
salted butter, softened

BLENDER OR FOOD PROCESSOR FITTED WITH STEEL BLADE

HANDHELD ELECTRIC MIXER

2 BAKING SHEETS, LINED WITH PARCHMENT PAPER

1 In a blender or food processor, combine the crystalized ginger and flour; pulse until the ginger is finely ground. (If you prefer, you can leave a few larger pieces for texture.)

2 In a medium bowl, using a handheld electric mixer on low speed, beat the butter until smooth. Increase the speed to high and beat for 1 minute. Add the flour mixture and mix by hand with a spoon. Once the dough comes together, form into a log 1½ inches (4 cm) in diameter. Wrap in parchment or waxed paper and refrigerate for at least 30 minutes, until firm, or for up to 3 days.

3 Preheat the oven to 300°F (150°C).

4 Using a sharp knife, slice the dough into rounds ¼ inch (0.5 cm) thick. Place the rounds on the prepared baking sheets, spacing them about 1 inch (2.5 cm) apart. Top each with a piece of crystalized ginger.

5 Bake one pan at a time on the middle rack of the preheated oven until the cookies are pale golden on the edges, about 18 to 22 minutes.

6 Let cool on the baking sheet for 5 minutes before transferring the cookies to a wire rack to cool completely.

TIPS

The crystalized ginger needs be dry, not moist and sticky. If yours is sticky, chop it into ¼-inch (0.5 cm) pieces and bake for 20 minutes in a preheated oven on the lowest setting — usually between 150°F and 170°F (70°C to 80°C).

Store the cookies in an airtight container at room temperature for up to 1 week.

My grandmother's signature cookie tasted like butterscotch and was impossibly chewy. She used a combination of white and brown sugars and loads of butter. This simplified version delivers the deep caramel notes I remember but relies on brown sugar only — the darker the better. The final result tastes more like salted caramel than my grandmother's original version, but I have yet to hear any complaints!

SALTED CARAMEL COOKIES

¹/₂ cup (115 g) salted butter, melted

•

³/₄ cup (180 g) packed dark brown sugar, plus 1 tablespoon (15 mL) for dipping

•

1 cup (140 g) self-rising flour (page 19)

BAKING SHEET, LINED WITH PARCHMENT PAPER

1 In a medium bowl, stir together the butter and ³/₄ cup (180 g) brown sugar until the sugar has dissolved and is no longer gritty. Add the flour and stir until well combined. The dough will be too soft to scoop at this point. Cover and refrigerate until firm, about 30 minutes, or overnight.

2 Preheat the oven to 350°F (180°C).

3 Form the dough into 2-inch (5 cm) balls. Place the 1 tablespoon (15 mL) brown sugar in a small bowl. Dip one side of each ball in the sugar and place on the prepared baking sheet with the sugared side up, 2 inches (5 cm) apart.

4 Bake on the middle rack of the preheated oven until the edges are golden, about 10 to 12 minutes.

5 Let cool on the baking sheet for 5 minutes before transferring the cookies to a wire rack to cool completely.

TIPS

In a rush? Skip the refrigeration in Step 1 and spoon 2 tablespoons (30 mL) dough per cookie directly onto the baking sheet (without dipping in sugar), spacing 3 inches (7.5 cm) apart. Bake on the middle rack of the preheated oven until the edges are golden, about 8 to 10 minutes. You'll get a flatter cookie, but it will taste just as good.

Store the cookies in an airtight container at room temperature for up to 1 week.

These are my go-to cookies for friends who can't eat dairy or gluten. They are easy to make, travel well and are light enough to end even a heavy meal. You can fancy them up by pressing a blanched almond into the top of each cookie before baking — but that would make four ingredients, so I promise not to tell anyone.

ITALIAN ALMOND COOKIES

1¼ cups (140 g)
almond flour

•

⅓ cup (75 g)
Citrus Sugar (page 21)

•

1 large egg white,
at room temperature

PREHEAT THE OVEN TO 350°F (180°C)

ELECTRIC MIXER

BAKING SHEET, LINED WITH PARCHMENT PAPER

1 In a medium bowl, whisk together the almond flour and citrus sugar.

2 In a separate medium bowl, using an electric mixer on high speed, beat the egg white until soft peaks form.

3 Gently stir the almond flour mixture into the egg white just until the dough comes together.

4 Using a 1-tablespoon (15 mL) cookie scoop or measuring spoon, scoop up some dough. Level the dough off by firmly pressing the scoop/spoon against the side of the bowl. Form into a ball, moistening your palms with water if it sticks to your hands. Place on the prepared baking sheet. Repeat with the remaining dough, spacing the balls 3 inches (7.5 cm) apart. Press each ball with a moistened palm to about ½ inch (1 cm) thick.

5 Bake on the middle rack of the preheated oven until light golden brown, about 12 to 14 minutes.

6 Let cool on the baking sheet for 5 minutes before transferring the cookies to a wire rack to cool completely.

TIPS

Almond flour spoils more quickly than wheat flour. Make sure to store it in an airtight container, away from light and heat, for up to 6 months. Even better, to keep your stash as fresh as possible, store it in the freezer for up to 1 year. To use, just measure out the amount you need and let it come to room temperature before baking.

Store the cookies in an airtight container at room temperature for up to 1 week.

Every year I ask my father what goodies he wants for Christmas. Every year he says the same thing: shortbread. I've learned to make a double — or triple — batch, because there are never enough.

SIMPLE SHORTBREAD

1 cup (225 g)
salted butter, softened

•

½ cup (110 g)
granulated sugar

•

2 cups (280 g)
all-purpose flour

2 BAKING SHEETS

1 In a large bowl, beat the butter with a wooden spoon until smooth and pale. Add the sugar gradually, about 1 tablespoon (15 mL) at a time, stirring after each addition until well incorporated.

2 Add the flour about one-quarter at a time, stirring well after each addition until a soft dough forms.

3 Divide the dough in half. Form each half into a log 2 inches (5 cm) in diameter. Wrap in parchment or waxed paper and refrigerate for at least 30 minutes, until firm, or for up to 3 days.

4 Preheat the oven to 300°F (150°C). Remove the dough from the refrigerator and let stand for 10 minutes at room temperature.

5 Using a sharp knife, slice the dough into rounds ¼ inch (0.5 cm) thick and place them ½ inch (1 cm) apart on the baking sheets.

6 Bake, one sheet at a time, on the middle rack of the preheated oven for 25 to 30 minutes or until slightly golden on the edges but still pale on top.

7 Transfer the cookies to a wire rack to cool completely.

TIPS

The dough in Step 3 can be frozen for up to 3 months. In Step 4, increase the standing time to 30 minutes, or until the dough is still firm but won't break when sliced.

The cookies can be stored in an airtight container in the refrigerator for up to 2 weeks or in the freezer for up to 4 months.

My mother never wasted food. When she made a pie or tarts, she'd gather up all the bits of pastry, roll them into a strip, slather it with butter and then fill it with whatever sweet thing she had on hand. Occasionally she'd use jam, but most of the time her roly-polies were made with cinnamon and sugar. My recipe doesn't use pastry scraps, but I make them in honor of my practical mother and her cinnamon-scented kitchen.

CINNAMON ROLY-POLIES

1 sheet pie crust dough (about 7 ounces/200 g), defrosted if necessary

•

2 tablespoons (30 g) salted butter, softened

•

2 tablespoons (30 g) Cinnamon Sugar (page 20)

PREHEAT THE OVEN TO 350°F (180°C)

BAKING SHEET, LINED WITH PARCHMENT PAPER

1 On a lightly floured work surface, unroll the pastry. Using a sharp knife or pizza wheel, trim to form a square. Fold the square in half, then roll it into a 12- by 8-inch (30 by 20 cm) rectangle.

2 Spread the butter over the pastry and sprinkle with cinnamon sugar.

3 Starting at the short end, roll the pastry tightly into a log. Cut into 12 slices about ¾ inch (2 cm) thick. Place on the prepared baking sheet, spacing about 1 inch (2.5 cm) apart.

4 Bake on the middle rack of the preheated oven until the edges are golden but the centers are still pale, about 10 to 12 minutes.

5 Let the cookies cool completely on the baking sheet on a wire rack.

TIPS

If your pastry sheet is already a rectangle of the correct size, you can skip step 1. If you can't find pastry sheets at all, you can use a 9-inch (23 cm) unbaked pie crust (about 6 ounces/175 g).

Store the cookies in an airtight container at room temperature for up to 1 week.

These ice-cream sandwiches walk the line between cookies and cake. I'm not quite sure where the "pie" part comes in, but I'm not one to quibble when there's dessert involved. No matter how you categorize these, they're a treat few can resist.

WHOOPIE PIE ICE-CREAM SANDWICHES

2 cups (500 mL) single-flavor full-fat ice cream (see Tips), divided

•

3/4 cup (105 g) self-rising flour (see page 19)

•

3 tablespoons (45 g) salted butter, melted

PREHEAT THE OVEN TO 350°F (180°C)

BAKING SHEET, LINED WITH PARCHMENT PAPER

1 In a medium bowl, let 3/4 cup (175 mL) ice cream stand at room temperature until melted and fluid, about 15 to 20 minutes (return the remaining ice cream to the freezer). Add the flour and melted butter, stirring until smooth. Set aside for 5 minutes.

2 Using a 1 3/4-inch (4.5 cm) ice-cream scoop (about 1 1/2 tablespoons/22 mL), scoop up dough, running the scoop against the side of the bowl to level it off. Drop 8 mounds of dough on the prepared baking sheet, spacing them 2 inches (5 cm) apart.

3 Bake on the middle rack of the preheated oven until the tops of the cookies are dry, about 8 to 10 minutes.

4 Transfer the cookies to a wire rack to cool completely.

5 Once the cookies have cooled, place a scoop of the remaining ice cream on the bottom of one cooled cookie. Place a second cookie on top, with its bottom against the ice cream. Twist the top and bottom to stick the cookie together (do not press or the cookie will fall apart). Repeat with the remaining cookies and ice cream. Eat before the filling melts.

TIPS

These work best with full-fat ice cream that has just a few ingredients, not a lot of ripples, swirls or add-ins. Think chocolate, strawberry or vanilla. If you really want to use Rocky Road, save it for the ice cream used between the cookies.

Once assembled, the sandwiches can be frozen for up to 1 month. Let them stand at room temperature for about 10 minutes before eating.

There's a lot of confusion between macaroons and macarons. Macarons are the fancy French pastries that come in bright colors and sandwich decadent fillings. They are made with finely ground almonds, are notoriously fussy, and require far more than three ingredients. Macaroons (with two O's) are made with coconut, come together in minutes, and almost never, ever fail. Which one do you want to make?

CHEWY MACAROONS

6 cups (600 g) sweetened shredded coconut

•

1 can (14 oz or 300 mL) full-fat sweetened condensed milk

•

1 tablespoon (15 mL) vanilla extract

PREHEAT THE OVEN TO 325°F (160°C)

2 BAKING SHEETS, LINED WITH PARCHMENT PAPER

1 In a large bowl, stir together the coconut, condensed milk and vanilla until the coconut is well coated.

2 Drop in 1-tablespoon (15 mL) mounds onto the prepared baking sheets, spacing them about $1\frac{1}{2}$ inches (4 cm) apart.

3 Bake, one sheet at a time, on the middle rack of the preheated oven until lightly browned around the edges, about 10 to 12 minutes.

4 Let cool on the baking sheet on a wire rack for 5 minutes before transferring the macaroons to the rack to cool completely.

TIPS

Be sure to scrape out the tin of condensed milk. I find tiny spatulas (see page 13) ideal for this job. Simply pouring the milk from the can may leave behind a good 2 tablespoons (30 mL) and will adversely affect the final results.

Substitute $1\frac{1}{2}$ teaspoons (7 mL) pure almond extract for the vanilla if you want an almond taste.

The macaroons will be more uniform if you use a 1-tablespoon (15 mL) cookie scoop. Grease the inside of the scoop with cooking oil for quick release.

You'll probably need to bake 4 sheets of cookies for this recipe. Once you remove the cookies from the baking sheet, you can use the same sheet and parchment liner a second time. Make sure the sheet has cooled before adding the next round of cookies.

Store in an airtight container at room temperature for up to 1 week.

Coconut flour is a very thirsty gluten-free flour that soaks up liquid quickly. Once found only in health food stores, this sandy-textured flour has worked its way onto grocery store shelves and into a wide range of recipes. Unlike Chewy Macaroons (page 41), these cookies deliver a crisp texture, thanks in part to the coconut flour.

COCONUT COOKIES

$^1/_2$ *cup (65 g)*
coconut flour

•

$^1/_4$ *cup (55 g)*
granulated sugar

•

6 tablespoons (90 g)
salted butter, melted

PREHEAT THE OVEN TO 350°F (180°C)

BAKING SHEET, LINED WITH PARCHMENT PAPER

1 In a medium bowl, combine the coconut flour and sugar. Drizzle with the melted butter and stir to combine. The dough should have the texture of wet sand.

2 Scoop out 1 tablespoon (15 mL) dough and press it hard in your fist to form a ball. Place each ball on the prepared baking sheet, spacing them about 1 inch (2.5 cm) apart, and flatten with your hand to $^1/_2$ inch (1 cm) thick.

3 Bake on the middle rack of the preheated oven until the edges are light golden, about 8 to 10 minutes.

4 Let the cookies cool completely on the baking sheet on a wire rack (warm cookies will crumble).

TIPS

Cookies made with coconut flour tend to burn more easily
than cookies made with wheat or other nut flours. Keep an eye
on them during the last minute or two of baking.

Store the cookies in an airtight container at room temperature for up to 1 week.

These cookies taste a bit like Ferrero Rocher chocolates, only they're bigger. And chewier. And you don't have to fiddle with the wrapping. On the downside, they're bigger and chewier and you have immediate access because you don't have to fiddle with the wrapping. Since I'm not good at portion control — or any control, for that matter — I make small batches. If you have willpower, feel free to double the recipe.

CHOCOLATE HAZELNUT COOKIES

*1 cup (300 g)
chocolate hazelnut
spread*

•

*1 cup (140 g)
all-purpose flour*

•

*1 large egg,
at room temperature*

PREHEAT THE OVEN TO 350°F (180°C)

BAKING SHEET, LINED WITH PARCHMENT PAPER

1 In a medium bowl, combine the chocolate hazelnut spread, flour and egg until smooth. The dough will be quite thick.

2 Scoop out 2 tablespoons (30 mL) of the dough and roll to form a ball. Place on the prepared pan and repeat with the remaining dough, spacing the balls 2 inches (5 cm) apart. Using moistened palms, flatten the balls to $\frac{1}{2}$ inch (1 cm) thick.

3 Bake on the middle rack of the preheated oven until the cookies are set at the edges but the middle is still slightly soft, about 8 to 10 minutes.

4 Let cool on the baking sheet for 5 minutes before transferring the cookies to a wire rack to cool completely.

TIP

Store the cookies in an airtight container at room temperature for up to 1 week.

Oatmeal and raisins are a classic combination, whether they're swirled together warm and soft in your breakfast bowl or stuffed helter-skelter into a cookie jar. Of course, chocolate chips are an acceptable alternative — for cookies, not porridge (see Tips). When it comes to baked goods, I'm open to either option, so go ahead, surprise me.

OATMEAL RAISIN COOKIES

2 large bananas, mashed (about 1½ cups/375 mL)

•

1¾ cups (175 g) quick-cooking rolled oats

•

½ cup (75 g) raisins (see Tips)

PREHEAT THE OVEN TO 350°F (180°C)

BAKING SHEET, LINED WITH PARCHMENT PAPER

1 In a large bowl, combine the mashed bananas and oats. Stir in the raisins.

2 Form the dough into 2-inch (5 cm) balls and place 2 inches (5 cm) apart on the prepared baking sheet. Wet your fingers and flatten each cookie to 2 inches (5 cm) across.

3 Bake on the middle rack of the preheated oven until the cookies are golden on top and just set to the touch, about 12 to 15 minutes.

4 Let cool on the baking sheet for 5 minutes before transferring the cookies to a wire rack to cool completely.

TIPS

If your raisins are dry, plump them up first to help keep them moist and chewy. Place them in a small bowl with enough boiling water to cover. Let stand for 5 to 10 minutes. Drain well, pat dry and then proceed with the recipe.

Use ½ cup (95 g) chocolate chips instead of the raisins for a chocolatey twist.

These cookies don't keep as long as those made with flour. Store in an airtight container at room temperature for up to 2 days.

My friend Jane loves meringues. She's a minimalist at heart and these simple cookies suit her perfectly. Initially I thought she was missing out. Wouldn't she prefer them stuffed with chocolate chips or swirled into an Eton Mess (page 162)? No. Instead, she takes a Zen-like approach. She will pick one up and examine its delicate, cloudlike form before biting into the sugary pillow of contrasting textures. Thanks to her, I've come to appreciate the crisp outside that yields to a light but chewy inside — even without chocolate chips.

MERINGUES

2 large egg whites, at room temperature

•

1/4 teaspoon (1 mL) cream of tartar

•

1/2 cup (110 g) granulated sugar

PREHEAT THE OVEN TO 250°F (120°C)

ELECTRIC MIXER

2 BAKING SHEETS, LINED WITH PARCHMENT PAPER

1 In a large bowl, using an electric mixer on medium speed, beat the egg whites until frothy. Add the cream of tartar and continue whipping until soft peaks form. With the mixer running, gradually add the sugar, 1 tablespoon (15 mL) at a time. (Resist the urge to rush this process — it can take 2 to 3 minutes.) Once all the sugar has been added, increase the speed to high and beat until the egg whites are stiff and glossy, about 3 minutes.

2 Spoon 2-inch (5 cm) rounds onto the prepared baking sheets, spacing them about 1 inch (2.5 cm) apart.

3 Bake on racks placed in the upper and lower thirds of the preheated oven for 60 minutes or until crisp on the outside but still slightly soft inside. The meringues should be pale and peel off the parchment easily. Turn off the oven, stick a wooden spoon in the door to keep it slightly ajar, and leave the meringues in the oven to cool for at least 1 hour or overnight.

TIPS

Eggs separate most easily when cold but whip best at room temperature (see page 17).

The egg yolks can be used for Baba de Camelo (page 152).

Store the meringues in an airtight container at room temperature for up to 3 days. Do not refrigerate.

Remember when you were a kid and your mom wouldn't make you that one treat everyone else had, no matter how often you asked? And you asked so often you were finally told, "When you grow up and do your own cooking, you can make [insert name of treat] as often as you like." Well, I grew up, and I'm making these.

BUTTERSCOTCH HAYSTACKS

1 cup (190 g) butterscotch chips

•

1/2 cup (130 g) creamy peanut butter

•

2 1/2 cups (125 g) crunchy chow mein noodles

BAKING SHEET, LINED WITH PARCHMENT PAPER

1 In a large microwave-safe bowl, melt together the butterscotch chips and peanut butter in the microwave in 30-second intervals, stirring in between, until smooth. (Alternatively, melt them on the stove; see page 15 for details.)

2 Add the chow mein noodles by the handful, lightly crushing them to break the longer noodles. Stir to coat.

3 Using two forks, scoop 12 mounds, about 2 tablespoons (30 mL) each, onto the prepared baking sheet. Be sure to plunge the tines of the fork to the bottom of the bowl with each scoop to ensure that each haystack is evenly coated.

4 Let stand at room temperature until firm, about 20 minutes. If the room is warm, refrigerate for 10 to 15 minutes.

TIPS

You can substitute chocolate chips for the butterscotch chips.

Crunchy chow mein noodles can be found in the Asian section of most grocery stores.

Store the haystacks in an airtight container in the refrigerator for up to 1 week.

I always have wonton wrappers in the freezer. While I rarely make actual wontons, I often use the wrappers for baking, since they make quick, crispy tart shells. They also make a-nice-change-of-pace cookies when I'm craving something not too sweet but crunchy. These shallow-fried treats are light, crispy and sure to disappear quickly.

CITRUSY WONTON COOKIES

Canola oil, grapeseed
oil or peanut oil

•

12 wonton wrappers,
each 3 inches (7.5 cm)
square

•

2 tablespoons (30 g)
Citrus Sugar (page 21)

LARGE, DEEP, HEAVY-BOTTOMED SAUCEPAN OR DUTCH OVEN

CANDY/DEEP-FRY THERMOMETER (OPTIONAL)

TONGS

WIRE RACK PLACED OVER A BAKING SHEET LINED WITH PAPER TOWELS

1 Cut the wonton wrappers in half from corner to corner to form triangles.

2 Pour enough oil into the saucepan to come 2 inches (5 cm) up the sides, being sure to leave enough space to more than accommodate the amount of oil that will be displaced when the wontons are added. Heat over medium heat until the oil instantly bubbles and a tiny piece of wonton rises to the top when it is dropped in, or the temperature on a candy/deep-fry thermometer reads 375°F (190°C).

3 Working in batches, gently place 3 to 4 wonton triangles in the hot oil, making sure you don't overcrowd the pan. Cook for 30 seconds. Using tongs, flip the wontons over and cook until golden brown, about 15 to 30 seconds. Using the tongs, remove the triangles and place on the prepared wire rack. Sprinkle immediately with citrus sugar.

4 Continue until all the wontons are cooked. Enjoy while warm and crispy.

TIPS

If the wonton triangles begin to cook more slowly, you might have to let the oil come back to temperature. Let it heat for 2 or 3 minutes, then retest with a scrap of wonton. Conversely, if the triangles are cooking too quickly or burning, reduce the heat and remove the pan from the element for a minute or two to let the oil cool down.

These cookies are best eaten right away and don't store well.

BARS & SQUARES

These squares were inspired by the popular popcorn that combines savory Cheddar and sweet caramel. Since I can't be trusted around a big bag of the popcorn, I thought I'd do damage control with a small pan of squares. I was wrong. Every time I walk by, the pan shrinks by a square or two.

CHICAGO-MIX SQUARES

1 package (6.6 oz/187 g) Cheddar-flavored fish crackers

•

1 package (8 oz/200 g) toffee bits, such as Skor or Heath (about 1 1/3 cups/325 mL)

•

1 can (14 oz or 300 mL) full-fat sweetened condensed milk

PREHEAT THE OVEN TO 350°F (180°C)

8-INCH (20 CM) SQUARE METAL BAKING PAN, LINED WITH PARCHMENT PAPER (SEE TIPS)

1 Place the crackers in a resealable plastic bag. Crush with a rolling pin or mallet until about the size of the toffee bits.

2 In a large bowl, combine the crushed crackers and toffee bits. Pour the condensed milk over top and stir until coated.

3 Press the mixture evenly into the prepared pan.

4 Bake on the middle rack of the preheated oven until the edges are golden and the center is bubbling, about 25 to 30 minutes.

5 Let cool completely in the pan on a wire rack. Once cooled, remove from the pan, using the parchment liner, and cut into squares.

TIPS

To get the parchment to fit neatly into the pan, crumple a sheet of the paper, wet it under running water, and shake off the excess. This will make the parchment pliable. Line the pan, pushing the parchment into the corners. Pat dry with a clean towel before filling.

Store the squares in an airtight container at room temperature for up to 1 week.

This is a variation of my Great-Aunt Bess's recipe, which was sweet and crunchy but fell apart no matter how hard we pressed it into the pan. We used to sit around the table with the pan hot from the oven and dig in with spoons. It didn't matter that we burned the roofs of our mouths — we couldn't resist its charms! This version holds together better, thanks to heating the butter and brown sugar. I'm still tempted to eat it right from the pan with a spoon — just for old time's sake — but there's no longer a need.

BUTTERY OATMEAL SQUARES

2 cups (200 g)
quick-cooking rolled oats

•

*½ cup (115 g)
salted butter, softened*

•

*¾ cup (180 g)
packed brown sugar*

PREHEAT THE OVEN TO 350°F (180°C)

8-INCH (20 CM) SQUARE METAL BAKING PAN, LINED WITH PARCHMENT PAPER

1 Place the oats in a medium bowl. Set aside.

2 In a small saucepan, heat the butter and brown sugar over medium heat, stirring constantly, until boiling. Boil, stirring constantly, for 1 minute. Pour over the oats, stirring to combine.

3 Press the mixture firmly and evenly into the prepared pan.

4 Bake on the middle rack of the preheated oven for 20 minutes. The mixture will bubble at the edges.

5 Let cool in the pan on a wire rack for 15 minutes. Score with a knife into 16 squares. Let cool completely, then remove from the pan, using the parchment liner, and cut along the scored lines.

TIPS

Store the squares in an airtight container at room temperature for up to 1 week.

These squares freeze really well. If you want to use them for school snacks, wrap individual squares in plastic wrap, place in a resealable freezer bag, and freeze. Pop individual frozen squares into lunch bags. They'll be defrosted by snack time.

What's better than a treat featuring chocolate and nuts? How about a no-bake treat featuring chocolate and nuts that comes together in minutes, doesn't make too much of a mess and requires only one bowl? Bonus: it still requires only three ingredients. I'd say we have a winner here.

CHOCOLATE ALMOND CRUNCHIES

1 1/2 cups (285 g) bittersweet (dark) chocolate chips

•

1/2 cup (130 g) creamy almond butter

•

4 cups (120 g) corn flakes cereal

8-INCH (20 CM) SQUARE BAKING PAN, LINED WITH PARCHMENT PAPER

1 In a large microwave-safe bowl, heat the chocolate chips in the microwave on High in 30-second intervals, stirring in between, until three-quarters of the chips have melted. Stir gently until all the chips have melted. (Alternatively, melt them on the stove. See page 15 for details.)

2 Add the almond butter, stirring until smooth. Fold in the cereal.

3 Press the mixture firmly and evenly into the prepared pan.

4 Cover and refrigerate until set, about 1 hour. Remove from the pan, using the parchment liner, and cut into squares.

TIPS

You can substitute peanut butter for the almond butter.

Store the crunchies in an airtight container at room temperature for up to 1 week.

In university I went through a homemade granola bar phase. They were portable and sweet, and kept me going between classes. The only problem was that they fell apart — I often ended up eating them with a spoon stolen from the cafeteria. These no-bake bars stick together. Not only are they perfect for when I'm on the go, they keep me honest.

NUTTY GRANOLA BARS

2¹/₂ cups (250 g)
granola

•

¹/₂ cup (130 g)
creamy almond butter

•

¹/₂ cup (125 mL)
corn syrup

8-INCH (20 CM) SQUARE METAL BAKING PAN, LINED WITH PARCHMENT PAPER

1 Place the granola in a large bowl. Set aside.

2 In a small saucepan over medium heat, heat the almond butter and corn syrup, stirring constantly, until melted and smooth, about 3 minutes. Make sure the mixture is warm but not boiling.

3 Pour the almond butter mixture over the granola and stir to coat.

4 Press the granola mixture evenly into the prepared pan. Cover and refrigerate until firm, about 30 minutes. Remove from the pan, using the parchment liner, and cut into bars.

TIPS

You can vary these bars by changing the granola or the nut butter. Try cashew, peanut or even seed butter for a change of pace.

Store the granola bars in an airtight container in the refrigerator for up to 1 week.

My mom hates nuts in brownies. I love them. Her objection isn't the taste; it's the texture. In her opinion, brownies shouldn't crunch. This recipe provides the perfect compromise. Thanks to chocolate hazelnut spread, she gets a moist, uncluttered brownie, while I get the nutty flavor I adore. But yesterday's solutions are today's problems: now that we agree on the brownies, we have to learn to share.

CHOCOLATE HAZELNUT BROWNIES

2¹/₂ cups (750 g) chocolate hazelnut spread, divided

•

3 large eggs, at room temperature

•

³/₄ cup (105 g) all-purpose flour

PREHEAT THE OVEN TO 350°F (180°C)

8-INCH (20 CM) SQUARE METAL BAKING PAN, LINED WITH PARCHMENT PAPER

1 In a large bowl, combine 1¹/₂ cups (450 g) chocolate hazelnut spread, eggs and flour. Mix until well combined.

2 Spread the batter evenly in the prepared pan.

3 Bake on the middle rack of the preheated oven until a tester comes out with only a few crumbs attached, about 25 minutes.

4 Let cool in the pan on a wire rack. Remove from the pan, using the parchment liner. Frost the top of the cooled brownies with the remaining chocolate hazelnut spread and cut into squares.

TIP

Store the brownies in an airtight container at room temperature for up to 4 days.

I grew up with those good ol' familiar plain marshmallow crispy squares. They were sweet and sticky and utterly predictable. Then once — and only once — Mom made them with chocolate marshmallows. I was hooked. For some reason chocolate marshmallows never appeared in our grocery store again, and we reverted to the traditional recipe, but I still longed for the chocolate version. Eventually I got smart. If I couldn't get the chocolate from the marshmallows, why not get the chocolate from the cereal? Problem solved.

COCOA SQUARES

¼ cup (60 g) salted butter

•

10 ounces (270 g) marshmallows (about 40 large; see Tips)

•

6 cups (240 g) chocolate puffed cereal, such as Cocoa Puffs

8-INCH (20 CM) SQUARE BAKING PAN, BUTTERED

1 In a large microwave-safe bowl, heat the butter and marshmallows in the microwave on High in 30-second intervals, stirring in between, until melted. (Alternatively, melt the butter in a large saucepan over low heat. Add the marshmallows and stir until melted. Remove from the heat.)

2 Stir in the cereal, mixing until well coated.

3 Spoon into the prepared pan. Using a buttered spatula, press the mixture firmly into the pan, flattening the top evenly.

4 Let cool completely, then cut into squares with a sharp knife.

TIPS

If you have only mini-marshmallows on hand, you'll need about 4 cups (1 L).

For easy cleanup, have a sink of hot, soapy water ready. As soon as you have pressed the mixture into the pan, pop the bowl, spoon and spatula into the sink and let them soak for 5 minutes. The sticky marshmallow will wash right off.

These squares are best when eaten the day they are made, but leftovers can be stored in an airtight container at room temperature for up to 3 days.

When I was a kid, I escaped to sleep-away camp for one carefree week each summer. The highlight of this adventure was the night we slept outside under the stars. Dinner was always the same: sloppy joes, followed by decadent s'mores that the campers assembled themselves. More chocolate chips ended up on the ground than in our dessert. If we didn't burn our fingers on the embers, we got scalded by molten marshmallows. It was glorious! Today I make a neater, more predictable version, but in my heart I'm dusting ashes off the graham crackers and licking the foil clean when no one is looking.

INDOOR S'MORES

8 graham cracker squares

•

Two 1.7-ounce (50 g) chocolate bars that can be broken into squares (see Tip)

•

4 large marshmallows

PREHEAT THE OVEN TO 400°F (200°C)

BAKING SHEET, LINED WITH PARCHMENT PAPER

1 Place 4 graham squares on the prepared baking sheet. Break the chocolate into pieces just smaller than a graham cracker square. Center the chocolate on top of each square. Place a marshmallow on top of the chocolate.

2 Bake on the middle rack of the preheated oven until the marshmallows are puffed up and golden brown, about 3 to 5 minutes.

3 Using a spatula, place the hot s'mores bottoms on a serving plate. Immediately top each with one of the remaining graham cracker squares. Press down gently to stick the marshmallow and chocolate together. Enjoy warm.

TIP

You can use any flavor of chocolate bar you like.
Try white chocolate, milk chocolate or bars with caramel centers.

CAKES, MUFFINS & QUICK BREADS

This simple cake is the perfect companion for a hot cup of tea. It's moist, not too sweet and can be fancied up with a bit of Chantilly Cream (page 206) if you're so inclined.

CITRUS ALMOND CAKE

4 large eggs, separated and brought to room temperature (see Tips)

•

1 cup (200 g) Citrus Sugar (page 21)

•

1$\frac{1}{3}$ cups (150 g) almond flour

PREHEAT THE OVEN TO 350°F (180°C)

ELECTRIC MIXER

8-INCH (20 CM) ROUND CAKE PAN, LINED WITH PARCHMENT PAPER (SEE PAGE 13 FOR A LINING TIP)

1 In a medium bowl, using an electric mixer on high speed, beat the egg yolks and sugar until smooth and pale, about 2 minutes. Stir in the almond flour until well combined. Wash and dry the beaters.

2 In a large bowl, using the electric mixer on high speed, beat the egg whites until stiff peaks form. Fold a third of the egg whites into the almond flour mixture. Fold the almond flour mixture into the remaining whites, until smooth. Pour the batter into the prepared pan and smooth the top.

3 Bake on the middle rack of the preheated oven until golden on top and firm to the touch, about 25 to 35 minutes.

4 Let cool completely in the pan on a wire rack. Remove from the pan, using the parchment liner. Slice and serve.

TIPS

Eggs separate most easily when cold but whip up best at room temperature. Separate eggs while the oven preheats and by the time you're ready to whip the whites, they should be at the ideal temperature.

Store the cake in an airtight container at room temperature for up to 3 days.

I learned about this simple, dense fruit cake from an Irish friend while living in Australia, so in my mind it's an international dish. The original version called for currants and golden raisins soaked overnight in black tea. I've amped up the fruit flavors by using orange juice and a mix of dried berries.

BARM BRACK

2 cups (300 g)
mixed dried fruit
(see Tips)

•

1½ cups (375 mL)
orange juice

•

1½ cups (210 g)
self-rising flour (page 19)

PREHEAT THE OVEN TO 275°F (140°C)

FINE-MESH SIEVE

8-INCH (20 CM) ROUND CAKE PAN, LINED WITH PARCHMENT PAPER (SEE PAGE 13 FOR A LINING TIP)

1 In a medium bowl, cover the dried fruit with the orange juice. Cover and refrigerate for at least 8 hours or overnight.

2 Drain the fruit through a fine-mesh sieve over a medium bowl, reserving the liquid.

3 Place the flour in a large bowl. Add the drained fruit, tossing to coat. Pour the reserved liquid over the flour mixture and stir just until combined. Spoon the batter into the prepared pan, spreading it evenly.

4 Bake on the middle rack of the preheated oven until the cake is golden and a tester inserted in the center comes out clean, about 75 to 90 minutes.

5 Let cool completely in the pan on a wire rack. Remove from the pan, using the parchment liner, before slicing.

TIPS

I use a packaged mix of dried fruit that includes cranberries, blueberries and cherries. You can also use raisins, dried currants, dried apricots or dates.

If you don't have an 8-inch (20 cm) round pan, use a 9- by 5-inch (23 by 12.5 cm) loaf pan instead.

Store the barm brack in an airtight container at room temperature for up to 1 week.

Cakes bejeweled with maraschino cherries and pineapple rings were all the rage in the 1950s and are enjoying a retro resurgence these days. To stay within the three-ingredient limit, I'm ditching the cherries. And because I'm a bit lazy, I'm using pineapple tidbits instead of rings, so I don't have to slice them. To make up for the cut corners, this version is loaded with pineapple, so you can enjoy its sweetness in every bite.

PINEAPPLE UPSIDE-DOWN CAKE

1 can (19 oz/540 mL) pineapple tidbits (with juice), divided

•

1¼ cups (275 g) granulated sugar, divided

•

2 cups (280 g) self-rising flour (page 19)

PREHEAT THE OVEN TO 350°F (180°C)

FINE-MESH SIEVE

8-INCH (20 CM) ROUND PAN, GENEROUSLY BUTTERED

1 Thoroughly drain the pineapple through a fine-mesh sieve over a medium bowl, reserving the juice (about 14 tablespoons/200 mL).

2 In a medium saucepan over medium heat, bring ¼ cup (55 g) sugar and 1 cup (250 mL) well-drained pineapple tidbits to a boil, stirring occasionally, until the syrup is light amber, about 5 to 10 minutes. Pour into the prepared pan. Spread to distribute evenly over the bottom of the pan.

3 In a large bowl, combine the flour and remaining sugar. Stir in the remaining pineapple (about 2 cups/480 mL) and the reserved juice, just until combined.

4 Spoon the batter into the prepared pan, being careful to keep the sugared pineapple evenly dispersed. Spread the batter gently to level it.

5 Bake on the middle rack of the preheated oven until a tester inserted in the center comes out clean, about 50 to 60 minutes.

6 Let cool in the pan on a wire rack for 10 minutes. Place a plate upside down over the cake pan, then flip them both over to turn out the cake onto the plate. Serve warm or at room temperature.

TIP

Store the leftover cake in an airtight container at room temperature for up to 3 days.

Icebox cakes have been around for almost a century, making them one of the original convenience foods. While the variations are endless, the basic principle remains the same: rich cream turns crisp cookies into stacks of soft, cakelike decadence. This version produces individual parfaits, which are perfect for serving to guests.

LEMON GINGER ICEBOX PARFAITS

1 cup (250 mL)
cold heavy or whipping
(35%) cream

•

½ cup (125 mL)
lemon curd

•

19 gingersnaps,
about 2 inches (5 cm)
in diameter

ELECTRIC MIXER

SIX 4- TO 6-OUNCE (125 TO 188 ML) GLASSES, WIDE ENOUGH TO ACCOMMODATE A GINGERSNAP

1 In a medium bowl, using an electric mixer on high speed, whip the cold cream until stiff peaks form.

2 In a small bowl, stir the lemon curd until smooth. Fold in a heaping spoonful of whipped cream. Fold the lemon curd into the remaining whipped cream.

3 For each parfait, place 1 tablespoon (15 mL) lemon cream in the bottom of a glass. Place one cookie on top of the cream and press gently to adhere. Place 1 tablespoon (15 mL) lemon cream in the center of the cookie. Repeat the layers of lemon cream and cookies until you have a total of 3 cookies, finishing with the lemon cream.

4 Crumble the remaining cookie and sprinkle over the top of each parfait. Cover and chill in the refrigerator until the cookies soften, at least 6 hours, or up to 3 days. Serve chilled.

TIPS

Cream whips best when cold. If your kitchen is warm, pop the bowl and beaters into the refrigerator for 10 minutes. While the bowl and beaters are chilling, pop the cream into the freezer. It should whip without issue.

To freeze, cover the parfaits with plastic wrap and store for up to 1 month. Just let them thaw in the refrigerator overnight before serving.

For my sister's wedding we made 13 Chocolate Chip Icebox Cakes, one for each table. Since the event was cause for celebration, we dipped the cookies in generous portions of Irish cream whiskey liqueur before layering them with whipped cream. Even without the alcohol, this family-friendly version of her wedding dessert is simple but decadent. And definitely worthy of any party.

CHOCOLATE CHIP ICEBOX CAKE

3 cups (750 mL) cold heavy or whipping (35%) cream

•

½ cup (65 g) confectioners' (icing) sugar

•

3 packages (each 10 oz/300 g) chocolate chip cookies (about forty 2-inch/5 cm cookies)

ELECTRIC MIXER

10-INCH (25 CM) SERVING PLATE OR CAKE STAND

1 In a large bowl, using an electric mixer on low speed, combine the cold cream and confectioners' sugar. Slowly increase the speed to high and beat until stiff peaks form.

2 Spread ¼ cup (60 mL) whipped cream in a 9-inch (23 cm) circle on the serving plate, leaving a 1-inch (2.5 cm) border around the edge of the plate. Arrange the cookies over the cream in a single layer (you'll need about 10 cookies).

3 Spread a quarter of the remaining whipped cream evenly over the cookies. Top with a second layer of cookies. Continue layering the cookies and cream until there are four layers of cookies, then finish with a layer of cream. Smooth the top of the cake. Crumble a few remaining cookies and sprinkle over the top. (A few cookies might still be left in the bag. Enjoy them as a reward for work well done, or crumble them up and pile them on top of the cake — your choice.)

4 Insert toothpicks around the edges of the cake and a few in the center, leaving 1 inch (2.5 cm) of toothpick exposed (this will prevent the plastic wrap from touching the whipped cream). Drape a long strip of plastic wrap over the top and gently secure it under the plate. Repeat with a second strip of plastic wrap, going in the opposite direction. Don't wrap tightly, or the toothpicks will pierce the plastic. Refrigerate until the cookies soften, at least 6 hours, or overnight.

TIP

Leftover cake can be rewrapped and refrigerated for up to 3 days, or frozen for up to 1 month.

When I was growing up, no-bake cheesecakes involved cream cheese and a tub of Cool Whip. While I can't claim this version is health food, it is more natural than the 70s version I was raised on. White chocolate holds the secret to this recipe, providing some sweetness as well as structure.

WHITE CHOCOLATE CHEESECAKE

1¹/₂ cups (375 mL) cold heavy or whipping (35%) cream

•

7 ounces (200 g) white chocolate, chopped, plus ¹/₂ ounce (15 g) for shaving (optional)

•

8 ounces (250 g) cream cheese, softened and cubed

ELECTRIC MIXER

8-INCH (20 CM) ROUND CAKE PAN, LINED WITH PARCHMENT PAPER (SEE PAGE 13 FOR A LINING TIP)

1 In a medium bowl, using an electric mixer on high speed, whip the cold cream until stiff peaks form. Cover and refrigerate until ready to use.

2 In a large microwave-safe bowl, heat the chopped chocolate in the microwave on High in 15-second intervals, stirring in between, until smooth. (Alternatively, melt it on the stove. See page 15 for details.)

3 Add the cream cheese to the chocolate and, using the electric mixer on medium speed, beat until smooth, about 1 to 2 minutes.

4 Fold the whipped cream into the cream cheese mixture. Spread evenly in the prepared pan and smooth the top.

5 Cover and refrigerate until firm enough to cut, about 1 hour. Remove from the pan, using the liner, before slicing. Sprinkle the top with shaved chocolate, if using (see Tips).

TIPS

For Chocolate Cheesecake, use bittersweet (dark) chocolate in place of the white.

To make chocolate shavings, draw the blade of a vegetable peeler down the edge of the chocolate to create flat, thin shavings.

Out of chocolate but have chocolate chips on hand? No problem. This recipe is a rare instance where you can substitute chips for real chocolate.

Since this is a no-bake cheesecake, it is softer than its baked counterparts. If, after an hour in the refrigerator, you find it challenging to slice, pop it in the freezer for 30 to 60 minutes.

Leftovers can be covered and stored in the refrigerator for up to 1 week.

Mug cakes are dangerous. Faced with spending an hour waiting for a full-sized cake to bake, my lazy gene kicks in and the craving eventually passes. But knowing I can produce a single serving of cake in mere minutes? This could become an issue.

CHOCOLATE MUG CAKE

1 large egg,
at room temperature

•

¼ cup (35 g)
confectioners'
(icing) sugar

•

2 tablespoons (10 mL)
unsweetened cocoa
powder

ONE 8-OUNCE (250 ML) MICROWAVE-SAFE MUG

1 In the mug, whisk together the egg, confectioners' sugar and cocoa powder.

2 Microwave on High for 45 seconds. The cake should begin to pull away from the sides of the mug and the top should look dry and spring back when tapped lightly. If it's not done, continue cooking in 15-second intervals.

3 Let cool for 5 minutes. Eat warm.

TIP

The timing will vary, depending on your microwave and mug. Handmade pottery mugs tend to be thicker and can take slightly longer to cook the cake. Once you find the right mug and timing, make a note in the margin.

If you like my Peanut Butter Cookies (page 28), this delivers the same taste but in cake form. Plus it's ready in no time. I've got you covered.

PEANUT BUTTER MUG CAKE

3 tablespoons (105 g) creamy peanut butter

•

2 tablespoons (30 g) granulated sugar

•

1 large egg, at room temperature

ONE 12-OUNCE (375 ML) MICROWAVE-SAFE MUG

1 In the mug, whisk together the peanut butter, sugar and egg until smooth.

2 Microwave on High for 60 seconds. The cake should begin to pull away from the sides of the mug and the top should look dry and spring back when tapped lightly. If it's not done, continue cooking in 15-second intervals.

3 Let cool until set, about 10 to 15 minutes. Eat warm.

TIPS

If you aren't sure how big your mug is, fill it with water and then pour the water into a measuring cup.

For even cooking, pick a tall, round mug with straight sides. Fat, squat mugs might overflow, while those with tapered sides can produce mug cakes with gooey bottoms.

I tell myself this is a romantic gesture — mug cakes for two — only I end up eating them both and cleaning up the evidence. Fortunately, mug cakes don't require a lot of work when it comes to covering one's tracks.

CHOCOLATE HAZELNUT MUG CAKES FOR TWO

1 large egg, at room temperature

•

2/3 cup (200 g) chocolate hazelnut spread

•

1/4 cup (35 g) all-purpose flour

TWO 12-OUNCE (375 ML) MICROWAVE-SAFE MUGS

1 In a small bowl, whisk together the egg and chocolate hazelnut spread until smooth. Whisk in the flour until smooth.

2 Divide the batter equally between the mugs.

3 Microwave both mugs on High for 1 minute and 15 seconds. The cakes should begin to pull away from the sides of the mugs and the tops should look dry and spring back when tapped lightly. If they're not done, continue cooking in 15-second intervals.

4 Let cool until set, about 10 to 15 minutes. Eat warm.

TIPS

For even cooking, pick tall, round mugs with straight sides.
Fat, squat mugs might overflow, while those with tapered sides can produce mug cakes with gooey bottoms.

Bigger mugs allow for expansion and reduce the risk of overflow.
If you don't have large mugs, use standard mugs (at least 8 oz/250 mL) and place them on a plate to catch any spills.

Sometimes you zig, sometimes you zag. Baking is rarely a straight course, and this recipe serves as a reminder. I set out to make a simple raspberry-studded loaf but got carried away with the fruit. The berries added far too much moisture to the mix. As a result, the loaf emerged from the oven dry on the outside but soggy and sunken in the middle. But I was determined. Changing tack, I took another route — I made muffins. These aren't too sweet and have a fresh zing from the berries.

RASPBERRY ICE-CREAM MUFFINS

2 cups (500 mL) good-quality vanilla ice cream (see Tips)

•

1 cup (140 g) raspberries, fresh or frozen, divided

•

1¹⁄₂ cups (210 g) self-rising flour (page 19)

PREHEAT THE OVEN TO 350°F (180°C)

12-CUP MUFFIN PAN, LINED WITH LIGHTLY GREASED PAPER LINERS

1 In a medium bowl, let the ice cream stand at room temperature until it's the texture of soft-serve ice cream, about 10 to 20 minutes. Stir until it's smooth but not liquid.

2 Set aside 12 raspberries.

3 In another medium bowl, combine the remaining raspberries and flour; toss to coat. Stir the flour mixture into the softened ice cream.

4 Spoon evenly into the wells of the prepared pan. Place one raspberry on top of each muffin.

5 Bake on the middle rack of the preheated oven until light golden and a tester inserted in the center comes out clean, about 25 minutes.

6 Let cool completely in the pan.

TIPS

This recipe works best with high-fat, full-sugar ice cream, not frozen yogurt, light ice cream or brands made with alternative sweeteners. When you pick up the carton, it should feel heavy for its size — this means the ice cream isn't full of air.

You can also try this recipe with good-quality full-fat chocolate ice cream.

Store the muffins in an airtight container in the refrigerator for up to 3 days.

I have a soft spot for this recipe. It uses often-neglected broken mandarin pieces, not the perfect plump whole segments that get all the attention. Citrus Sugar ramps up the orange flavor, but if you don't have any on hand, use plain granulated sugar (see Tips). The mandarin bits won't mind — they're happy to be of service.

MANDARIN MUFFINS

1 cup (200 g)
Citrus Sugar (page 21)

•

2 cups (280 g)
self-rising flour (page 19)

•

2 cans (each
10 oz/284 mL) broken
mandarin segments in
light syrup (with liquid)

PREHEAT THE OVEN TO 350°F (180°C)

12-CUP MUFFIN PAN, LINED WITH LIGHTLY GREASED PAPER LINERS

1 In a large bowl, combine the citrus sugar and flour. Add the mandarin segments, with liquid, and combine just until blended.

2 Spoon the batter evenly into the wells of the prepared pan.

3 Bake on the middle rack of the preheated oven until a tester inserted in the center comes out clean, about 20 to 25 minutes.

4 Let cool completely in the pan on a wire rack.

TIPS

If you don't have Citrus Sugar on hand, use 1 cup (220 g) granulated sugar and add the grated zest of an orange.

If you can't find broken mandarin pieces, drain whole segments, reserving the liquid, and roughly chop them into 3 or 4 pieces each. You want small bits distributed throughout the muffins.

Store the muffins in an airtight container in the refrigerator for up to 3 days.

You know something is good when your husband tastes it and then keeps wandering back into the kitchen "just to be sure." These simple pancakes come together in minutes, making them a practical option for breakfast, brunch or even those times when you feel like having breakfast for dinner.

BANANA PANCAKES

³/₄ cup (175 mL) mashed ripe banana (about 1 medium)

•

2 large eggs, at room temperature

•

¹/₂ cup (70 g) self-rising flour (page 19)

LARGE NONSTICK SKILLET, BUTTERED

1 In a medium bowl, whisk together the mashed banana and eggs until smooth. Stir in the flour until just incorporated.

2 Heat the skillet over medium heat. Working in batches, spoon 2 tablespoons (30 mL) batter into the hot skillet, being careful to leave space between the pancakes. Cook until bubbles form and the edges look dry, about 2 minutes. Flip with a spatula and cook until cooked all the way through and golden, about 2 minutes. Repeat with the remaining batter, adding more butter to the pan and adjusting the heat if needed.

3 Enjoy warm with your choice of pancake toppings.

TIPS

Ripe bananas work best in this recipe. If you have lots of ripe bananas on hand but can't use them all, freeze pre-mashed bananas for the future. Simply peel, mash and place in resealable plastic freezer-safe bags. Be sure to squeeze out the air before sealing, then label with the date and contents. They'll last in the freezer for up to 2 months.

Leftover pancakes can be wrapped and refrigerated for up to 5 days or frozen for up to 3 months. Just pop a frozen pancake in your toaster to reheat it and you're ready to go.

Christmas morning means fresh, piping-hot scones, not day-old ones, and not even hour-old ones! Only fresh-from-the-oven scones — and I'm in charge of them. These are a simplified version of our Christmas morning scones. The secret lies in the buttermilk and the folding.

BUTTERMILK SCONES

2 cups (280 g) self-rising flour (page 19)

•

½ cup (115 g) cold salted butter

•

1 cup (250 mL) buttermilk

PREHEAT THE OVEN TO 425°F (220°C)

BAKING SHEET, LINED WITH PARCHMENT PAPER

1 Place the flour in a large bowl. Using the large holes of a box grater, grate the butter over the flour. Toss to coat the butter with flour.

2 Pour the buttermilk over the flour mixture. Stir until most of the flour is absorbed.

3 Transfer to a floured work surface. Using your hands, pat the dough into a rectangle about 10 by 5 inches (25 by 12.5 cm). Starting at the short side, fold the dough in half. Flatten it slightly, give the rectangle a quarter-turn, then fold and flatten again. Repeat about 5 or 6 times. Pat the dough to ¾ inch (2 cm) thick. Cut into 12 squares. Place on the prepared baking sheet, spacing the squares about 1 inch (2.5 cm) apart.

4 Bake on the middle rack of the preheated oven until golden and puffed, about 12 to 15 minutes. Serve immediately.

TIPS

If you don't have buttermilk on hand, sour some milk instead. Place 1 tablespoon (15 mL) white vinegar in a measuring cup. Fill to the 1-cup (250 mL) line with milk. Stir and let stand for 5 minutes.

These scones are best eaten hot from the oven. If you want to make them ahead, place the cut dough on a baking sheet lined with parchment paper and freeze. Once frozen, transfer the scones to a resealable freezer bag and freeze for up to 3 months. When you're ready to bake, place them on a prepared baking sheet at room temperature while the oven preheats. Bake as directed, increasing the time to about 15 to 20 minutes.

PASTRIES, PIES & TARTS

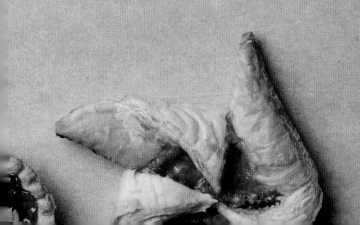

These pretty pastries are imposters. They resemble classic Danishes but are made with puff pastry. Their flashy spokes look challenging but require little more than some knife strokes. The only part of their appearance you can trust is the promise that they will taste delicious.

STRAWBERRY PINWHEELS

2 tablespoons (30 g) cream cheese, softened

•

2 tablespoons (30 mL) strawberry jam, divided

•

1 sheet puff pastry dough, 10 inches (25 cm) square, thawed if frozen (8 oz/225 g)

PREHEAT THE OVEN TO 375°F (190°C)

BAKING SHEET, LINED WITH PARCHMENT PAPER

1 In a small bowl, combine the cream cheese and 1 tablespoon (15 mL) strawberry jam. Set aside.

2 Place the pastry sheet on a lightly floured work surface. Using a sharp knife or pizza cutter, trim the rough edges, then cut the dough into 4 squares of about 5 inches (12.5 cm) each. Place on the prepared baking sheet, spacing them at least 2 inches (5 cm) apart.

3 Divide the cream cheese mixture evenly among the squares, placing a dollop in the center of each and spreading lightly to form a 2-inch (5 cm) circle.

4 Cut from each corner of the square toward the center, stopping at the cream cheese mixture. Fold the right side from each cut corner into the center, pressing the tip lightly into the cream cheese. Once the 4 "spokes" are folded in, place one-quarter of the remaining strawberry jam in the center, where all the tips come together. Repeat until you have 4 pinwheels.

5 Bake on the middle rack of the preheated oven until the pastry is golden brown, about 15 to 20 minutes. Enjoy warm from the oven.

TIP

This recipe can be doubled, but keep in mind that these pastries taste best the day they are made. Store leftovers in an airtight container in the refrigerator and eat the next day. You can reheat them in an oven preheated to 250°F (120°C) or a toaster oven until warmed through, about 10 to 15 minutes.

These pastries are a bit like tying shoelaces. The description is intimidating, but once you get your hands involved, it all makes sense. Best of all, unlike shoelaces, these won't come undone at an inconvenient moment.

MIXED BERRY DIAMONDS

½ cup (75 g) blueberries, fresh or frozen

•

2 tablespoons (30 mL) raspberry jam

•

2 sheets puff pastry dough, each 10 inches (25 cm) square, thawed if frozen (1 lb/455 g)

PREHEAT THE OVEN TO 375°F (190°C)

BAKING SHEET, LINED WITH PARCHMENT PAPER

1 In a medium bowl, combine the blueberries and raspberry jam. Set aside.

2 Place one sheet of dough on a lightly floured work surface. Using a sharp knife or pizza cutter, trim the rough edges of the sheet, then cut it into 4 squares of about 5 inches (12.5 cm) each. Working with one square at a time, fold in half on the diagonal to form a triangle. Starting ½ inch (1 cm) from the folded edge, cut a border along each of the short sides of the triangle all the way through both layers, stopping about ½ inch (1 cm) before the corner. Transfer to the prepared baking sheet. Unfold the pastry to create a square within a square.

3 Lift one corner of the outer square and fold it across the pastry until it aligns with the corner of the inner square on the opposite side. Repeat with the other corner of the outer square. You will have created a diamond with a twist at the top and bottom. Place 1 tablespoon (15 mL) blueberry mixture in the center. Repeat with the remaining dough until you have 8 pastries, spacing them at least 2 inches (5 cm) apart.

4 Bake on the middle rack of the preheated oven until the center is bubbling and the pastry is a deep golden brown all over, about 18 to 20 minutes.

5 Let cool slightly on the baking sheet on a wire rack. The pastries can be enjoyed warm or at room temperature.

TIP

These pastries are best enjoyed the day they are made. Leftovers can be stored an airtight container at room temperature for up to 1 day.

TIPS

For best results, choose a firm red apple that holds its shape when cooked, such as Honeycrisp, Gala, Fuji or Pink Lady.

You'll likely have some apple slices left over. You can eat them as is or stir them into yogurt for a change of pace at breakfast or snack time.

These pastries taste best the day they are made. Leftovers can be stored in an airtight container at room temperature for up to 1 day. If desired, reheat for 10 minutes in the muffin pan or on a baking sheet on the middle rack of an oven preheated to 250°F (120°C).

These striking pastries always draw compliments and are surprisingly easy to make. The only trick is to cut the apple slices thinly and cook them until they're soft enough to bend. Other than that, it's wrap and roll! But make sure not to tell your guests — try to convince them that you could have grown real roses faster, and see if it leverages you some help with post-dessert cleanup.

BAKED APPLE ROSES

1/4 cup (60 mL) raspberry jam

•

2 red apples, halved and sliced crosswise into half-moons 1/16 inch (2 mm) thick (see Tips)

•

1 sheet puff pastry dough, 10 inches (25 cm) square, thawed if frozen (8 oz/225 g)

PREHEAT THE OVEN TO 375°F (190°C)

12-CUP MUFFIN PAN

1 In a medium saucepan, combine the jam with 2 tablespoons (30 mL) water. Bring to a boil over medium heat, stirring occasionally. Remove from the heat and set aside.

2 Place the apple slices in the hot jam mixture and toss gently to coat.

3 Return the saucepan to medium heat and gently cook the apples for 2 minutes, stirring only enough to coat the slices, until they are soft enough to bend without breaking.

4 On a lightly floured work surface, fold the puff pastry dough in half and roll it out into a 12- by 9-inch (30 by 23 cm) rectangle. Cut the dough widthwise into 6 strips, each 12 by 1 1/2 inches (30 by 4 cm).

5 Using a fork or tongs, remove the apple slices one at a time from the jam mixture, shaking off any excess. Place an apple slice on the left end of each strip, so the edge with the red skin extends above the long edge of the pastry and the bottom is about halfway across it. Place a total of about 8 apple slices along the strip of pastry in the same way, overlapping their ends slightly.

6 Starting at one end, carefully roll up the dough strip jelly-roll-style, keeping the apple slices in place. Pinch the dough "stem" to seal, tuck it under the base and place the rose in one well of the muffin pan. Adjust the apple "petals" if they have shifted out of place. Repeat until you have 6 apple roses, spacing them apart in the muffin pan. Brush the tops with any remaining jam mixture.

7 Bake on the middle rack of the preheated oven until the pastry is golden and the apples are soft, about 40 to 45 minutes. Let stand for 10 minutes on a wire rack, then remove from the pan with a dull knife. Eat warm.

I'm iffy on the unadorned banana. But cover it in chocolate and caramel and wrap it in puff pastry? I'm so there. This is my simplified take on the classic English banoffee pie, which is banana cream pie with swirls of caramel and chocolate. What it lacks in cream it makes up for with caramel-filled chocolates. Of course, if you want to top it off with some Chantilly Cream (page 206), I won't complain.

BANOFFEE TRIANGLES

1 sheet puff pastry dough, 10 inches (25 cm) square, thawed if frozen (8 oz/225 g)

•

1 small ripe banana, sliced into 8 rounds about ¹/₂ inch (1 cm) thick

•

8 caramel-filled chocolate candy pieces, such as Rolos or Caramilk squares

PREHEAT THE OVEN TO 425°F (220°C)

BAKING SHEET, LINED WITH PARCHMENT PAPER

1 Place the pastry dough on a lightly floured work surface. Using a sharp knife or pizza cutter, cut the sheet into four 5-inch (12.5 cm) squares. Cut each square in half from corner to corner, making 8 triangles.

2 Place 1 banana slice just off center on each triangle. Top with a caramel chocolate. Fold the dough in half over the filling to form a smaller triangle. Using the tines of a fork, crimp the two unsealed edges. Place on the prepared baking sheet, spacing the triangles 2 inches (5 cm) apart.

3 Bake on the middle rack of the preheated oven until the pastry is golden all over, about 12 to 15 minutes. Transfer to a wire rack to cool slightly. Eat while the centers are still warm.

TIPS

You don't need to buy expensive chocolate caramels. I like Rolos or cubes of Caramilk here, but if you want to go gourmet, I won't stop you.

These treats should be eaten the day they are made. If quantity is an issue, make only as many as you can eat.

For such a simple pastry, this recipe has a lot of nicknames. I've heard palmiers, palm leaves, French hearts, glasses and even spectacles. Whatever you call them, these crispy, flaky treats will have you asking for more.

ELEPHANT EARS

$\frac{1}{2}$ *cup (110 g) granulated sugar, divided (approx.)*

•

1 sheet puff pastry dough, 10 inches (25 cm) square, thawed if frozen (8 oz/225 g)

•

2 ounces (60 g) bittersweet (dark) chocolate, chopped

PREHEAT OVEN TO 375°F (190°C)

2 BAKING SHEETS, LINED WITH PARCHMENT PAPER

WIRE RACK, PLACED OVER PARCHMENT PAPER

1 Dust a clean work surface with half the sugar. Place the pastry sheet on the sugar and sprinkle with additional sugar. Fold the pastry in half, sprinkle with more sugar, and roll it into a 12- by 8-inch (30 by 20 cm) rectangle, adding more sugar to the work surface or top of the pastry if it begins to stick (this will work some of the sugar into the dough).

2 Fold both long edges toward the center of the pastry, leaving a $\frac{1}{2}$-inch (1 cm) gap down the center. Then place one long side of the pastry on top of the other, folding along the center gap like closing a book. You will now have a strip of pastry that is 4 layers thick and measures approximately 2 inches (5 cm) wide and 12 inches (30 cm) long. Pat lightly to secure the folds.

3 Using a sharp knife, cut the pastry crosswise into slices $\frac{1}{2}$ inch (1 cm) thick, discarding the uneven ends. Dip the cut edges in sugar and place on the prepared baking sheets, spacing them at least 2 inches (5 cm) apart.

4 Bake on the middle rack of the preheated oven until the pastry is light gold on the edges and the centers are cooked, about 12 to 18 minutes. Transfer to the prepared wire rack to cool completely.

5 In a medium microwave-safe bowl, heat the chocolate in the microwave on High in 30-second intervals, stirring in between, until about three-quarters of the chocolate has melted. Stir gently until all the chocolate has melted. (Alternatively, melt it on the stove; see page 15 for details.) Let cool until slightly warm to the touch but still fluid.

6 Pour the chocolate into a resealable plastic bag and twist the open end to seal. Holding the bag over the pastries, snip a tiny piece from one corner. Moving back and forth over the pastries, gently squeeze the bag to drizzle the chocolate. Let the chocolate harden before eating.

Every holiday season I'm generously given jars of gourmet jam and wheels of cheese. I pay it forward by turning the gifts into hot appetizers — often gobbled down by the gift-givers. I'm now beginning to see a pattern . . .

BRIE AND BLUEBERRY BUNDLES

2 sheets puff pastry dough, each 10 inches (25 cm) square, thawed if frozen (1 lb/455 g)

•

3 ounces (90 g) Brie cheese, cut into eight $\frac{1}{2}$-inch (1 cm) cubes

•

3 tablespoons (45 mL) blueberry jam

PREHEAT THE OVEN TO 375°F (190°C)

12-CUP MUFFIN PAN

1 Place one sheet of dough on a lightly floured work surface. Using a sharp knife or pizza cutter, cut the sheet into four 5-inch (12.5 cm) squares.

2 Place a pastry square over one well of the muffin pan. Place a Brie cube in the center and press lightly to push the pastry into the well without breaking it. Place 1 teaspoon (5 mL) blueberry jam directly on top of the Brie. Fold the corners of the pastry into the center over the filling. Pinch the edges together where they touch to form four seams.

3 Repeat steps 1 and 2 with the second sheet of dough. You will have 8 bundles.

4 Bake in the preheated oven until the pastry is a deep gold all over, about 20 to 25 minutes.

5 Let cool in the pan on a wire rack for 5 minutes before removing. Eat warm.

TIPS

While I use blueberry jam, you can use any jam or jelly you like.
For a spicy twist, try hot red pepper jelly.

Store the bundles in an airtight container in the refrigerator for up to 3 days.

Do not rewarm these bundles in a microwave, or you will end up
with soggy pastry. Warm for 10 to 15 minutes on the middle rack
of an oven preheated to 250°F (120°C).

No one can agree on baklava. The Greeks and Turks both call it theirs, and some regions of Russia also stake a claim for its creation. I've tasted variations with almonds, pistachios and walnuts, and I've had it arrive at my table piping hot and swimming in syrup and even gobbled versions that were cold, dry and crumbly. This simplified version is a nod to the original. The fact that it's easier to make and has a higher nut-to-phyllo ratio are points no one can argue about.

MINI BAKLAVA BITES

1 box prebaked phyllo
pastry mini shells
(15 per box; see Tips)

•

1 cup (150 g) finely
chopped salted mixed
nuts (see Tips)

•

$^1/_2$ cup (125 mL) honey

PREHEAT THE OVEN TO 350°F (180°C)

1 Place the phyllo shells on a baking sheet.

2 In a small bowl, combine the nuts and honey (see Tips).

3 Spoon the filling evenly into the shells.

4 Bake on the middle rack of the preheated oven until the honey is bubbling and the nuts are fragrant, about 10 minutes.

5 Let cool slightly on the baking sheet on a wire rack. Enjoy slightly warm or at room temperature.

TIPS

Can't find mini phyllo cups? Make your own in minutes. Lay an 18- by 12-inch (46 by 30 cm) phyllo sheet on your work surface and brush with canola oil, olive oil or grapeseed oil. Place a second sheet on top and brush with oil. Fold in half lengthwise so you have an 18- by 6-inch (46 by 15 cm) stack four layers thick. Using a sharp knife or pizza cutter, cut the phyllo into fourteen 2$^1/_2$-inch (6 cm) squares, discarding scraps. Press the squares into 14 cups of a mini muffin pan. Bake on the middle rack of an oven preheated to 350°F (180°C) until pale golden, about 5 to 7 minutes. Let cool completely in the pan on a wire rack.

While you can use any combination of mixed nuts you like, almonds, walnuts and pistachios work well as a mix.

The honey should be runny in order to coat the nuts evenly. If your honey is thick, place it in a small microwave-safe bowl and microwave on High in 10-second intervals, stirring in between, until liquid.

Store in an airtight container at room temperature for up to 3 days.

These small pies contain fruit and almond butter, which means they're practically breakfast. While I won't stop you from enjoying one with your morning coffee, I'd like to point out that these also make a lovely dessert at the end of the day.

PEAR AND ALMOND PIES

2 sheets puff pastry dough, each 10 inches (25 cm) square, thawed if frozen (1 lb/455 g)

•

1/2 cup (130 g) almond butter

•

2 small ripe pears

PREHEAT THE OVEN TO 375°F (190°C)

BAKING SHEET, LINED WITH PARCHMENT PAPER

1 Place one sheet of dough on a lightly floured work surface. Using a sharp knife or pizza cutter, trim the rough edges of the sheet, then cut it into four 5-inch (12.5 cm) squares. Place on the prepared baking sheet, spacing them at least 2 inches (5 cm) apart. Repeat with the remaining dough, leaving the second set of squares on the work surface.

2 Cut out a 4-inch (10 cm) circle from the center of each square on the work surface, reserving them for another use. Using a finger dipped in water, moisten the edges of the pastry. Place a square with the circle removed on top of each of the solid squares, moistened edges together, creating a border.

3 Spread 2 tablespoons (30 mL) almond butter inside each circle.

4 Peel the pears. Slice them in half from top to bottom and remove the stem, core and seeds. Place cut side down on the cutting board and, starting about 1/2 inch (1 cm) from the stem end, thinly slice each half lengthwise, leaving the stem end intact to hold the fruit together. Using the palm of your hand, gently flatten the sliced pear to fan it out. Place the pear half, cut side down, on top of the almond butter within the pastry circle. Repeat with the remaining pear halves.

5 Bake on the middle rack of the preheated oven until the pastry is golden and the pears are tender, about 18 to 20 minutes.

6 Let cool slightly on the baking sheet. Eat warm.

TIP

The tarts are best enjoyed the day they are made.
Leftovers can be stored in an airtight container overnight.

When I was a child, one of the first bakery treats I remember was the oddly named Eccles cake. The name was fun to say and I could amuse myself by picking the bits of sugar off the top, but it was the baby raisins lurking inside that won me over. My mother tried to tell me they were currants, not raisins. I was so enamored by the concept of infant fruit that I refused to believe her. Today the bakery is no longer in business and I can't find Eccles cakes anywhere. So I created my own. Turns out Mom was right — they are filled with currants.

ECCLES CAKES

$^1/_2$ *cup (75 g)
dried currants*

•

$^1/_4$ *cup (50 g)
Citrus Sugar (page 21),
plus 1 tablespoon
(15 mL) for sprinkling*

•

*1 sheet puff pastry
dough, 10 inches (25 cm)
square, thawed if frozen
(8 oz/225 g)*

PREHEAT THE OVEN TO 425°F (220°C)

BAKING SHEET, LINED WITH PARCHMENT PAPER

1 In a small saucepan over medium heat, combine the currants, $^1/_4$ cup (50 g) sugar and 1 teaspoon (5 mL) water. Bring to a boil, stirring occasionally, then remove from the heat. Set aside to cool to room temperature.

2 Place the dough on a lightly floured work surface. Cut out four 5-inch (12.5 cm) circles, discarding the scraps or reserving them for another use.

3 Place one-quarter of the currant mixture in the center of one circle. Using a finger dipped in water, moisten the edges of the dough. Lift the edges up to the center to enclose the filling and then pinch to seal. Place the pastry, seal side down, on the prepared baking sheet. Taking care not to break the dough, gently press the pastry with a wet hand, flattening it enough to see the currants through the dough. Sprinkle with additional citrus sugar. Using a sharp knife, make 2 or 3 parallel slits in the top of the cake. Repeat until you have 4 cakes, spacing them 2 inches (5 cm) apart.

4 Bake on the middle rack of the preheated oven until the pastries are a deep golden brown, about 15 to 20 minutes.

5 Let cool on the pan on a wire rack. Enjoy warm or at room temperature.

TIP

The pastries can be stored in an airtight container
at room temperature for up to 3 days.

I can be impatient. While I love pie, I don't love how long it takes to bake or the suspense of wondering if I'll fall victim to the dreaded soggy bottom. Ready in a fraction of the time, these tarts not only satisfy my sense of urgency, they are good for the ego, since a light, flaky bottom crust is guaranteed.

CARAMEL APPLE TARTS

1 sheet puff pastry dough, 10 inches (25 cm) square, thawed if frozen (8 oz/225 g)

•

6 tablespoons (90 mL) dulce de leche, divided (see Tips)

•

1 firm apple, halved and sliced crosswise into half-moons $1/16$ inch (2 mm) thick (see Tips)

PREHEAT THE OVEN TO 375°F (190°C)

BAKING SHEET, LINED WITH PARCHMENT PAPER

1 Place the sheet of dough on a lightly floured work surface. Using a sharp knife or pizza cutter, trim the rough edges of the sheet, then cut into four 5-inch (12.5 cm) squares. Using a sharp knife, score the dough $1/2$ inch (1 cm) from the outer edges, creating a square within the square. Place the pastries on the prepared baking sheet, spacing them at least 2 inches (5 cm) apart.

2 Spread 1 tablespoon (15 mL) dulce de leche inside the score lines of each pastry. Arrange the apple slices over top, overlapping in a decorative pattern.

3 Place the remaining dulce de leche in a small microwave-safe bowl. Heat in the microwave on High in 10-second intervals, stirring in between, until warm and pourable. Using a fork, evenly drizzle the warm dulce de leche over the apple slices on each tart.

4 Bake on the middle rack of the preheated oven until the pastry is puffed and golden all over and the apple is tender, about 20 to 25 minutes.

5 Let cool slightly on the baking sheet on a wire rack for 5 to 10 minutes. Enjoy warm.

TIPS

If you don't have dulce de leche, use any thick caramel sauce.

Any firm apple that holds its shape when cooked will work well for these tarts. Try Honeycrisp, Granny Smith, Fuji or Gala.

This recipe can be doubled, but pastries are best the day they are made. Store leftovers in an airtight container in the refrigerator and eat the next day.

They say opposites attract. These tarts feature soft jam and crunchy almonds, and I like to think the contrasting textures hold the key to this ideal pairing. Then again, love is blind — the heart wants what the heart wants. Or, in this case, my mouth wants what my mouth wants.

MINI CHERRY TARTS

1 package frozen tart shells with foil liners (12 per box)

•

³/₄ cup (175 mL) cherry jam

•

¹/₄ cup (30 g) slivered almonds

PREHEAT THE OVEN TO 375°F (190°C)

1 Place the tart shells (in their liners) on a baking sheet.

2 Spoon about 1 tablespoon (15 mL) cherry jam into each shell. Evenly sprinkle the tops with slivered almonds.

3 Bake on the middle rack of the preheated oven until the pastry is golden and the jam is bubbling, about 15 to 20 minutes.

4 Transfer the tarts to a wire rack to cool. Serve slightly warm or at room temperature.

TIPS

Tart shells can be used straight from the freezer without defrosting. If using homemade shells, there's no need to freeze them first. Just make sure they are refrigerated for 30 minutes before filling and baking.

The tarts can be stored in an airtight container at room temperature for up to 3 days.

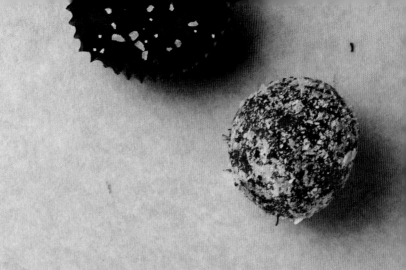

CHOCOLATE

When I was a kid, the day after Halloween was always candy-swap day. While no one wanted the kiss candies, chocolate bars were considered gold. Anything with peanuts ranked near the top of the chocolate-bar hierarchy. These two-bite peanut butter cups are a nod to one of the most coveted Halloween treats in my bag, but don't wait for October to make them. They're welcome in our house any time of year.

CHOCOLATE PEANUT BUTTER CUPS

8 ounces (225 g) bittersweet (dark) chocolate, chopped

•

¼ cup (65 g) peanut butter

•

Flaky sea salt

MINI MUFFIN PAN, LINED WITH 12 FOIL OR PARCHMENT PAPER LINERS

1 In a medium microwave-safe bowl, heat the chocolate in the microwave on High in 30-second intervals, stirring in between, until about three-quarters melted. Stir gently until completely melted. (Alternatively, melt it on the stove; see page 15 for details.) Spoon 1½ teaspoons (7 mL) chocolate into each of the liners. Set aside the remaining chocolate for topping (see Tips). Place the pan in the freezer to harden, about 10 minutes.

2 Spoon 1 teaspoon (5 mL) peanut butter into the center of each liner, keeping it away from the sides (see Tips). Evenly spoon the remaining chocolate (about 1½ teaspoons/7 mL per cup) over the peanut butter, coating it and adding enough to create a flat top. Sprinkle with a pinch of sea salt flakes.

3 Transfer to the refrigerator to harden for at least 10 minutes before eating.

TIPS

Although they come in fancy colors and patterns, paper liners tend to shred when you peel them away from the chocolate. Look for foil-lined papers or liners made of parchment, which are sturdier and will release the chocolate cup without any arguments.

If you need to remelt the chocolate, place it in a microwave-safe bowl and microwave on High in 15-second intervals, stirring in between, until liquid again.

If the peanut butter is sticking to the measuring spoon, slide it off with a small spoon, a mini spatula or the tip of a dinner knife.

Store the peanut butter cups in an airtight container in the refrigerator for up to 2 weeks.

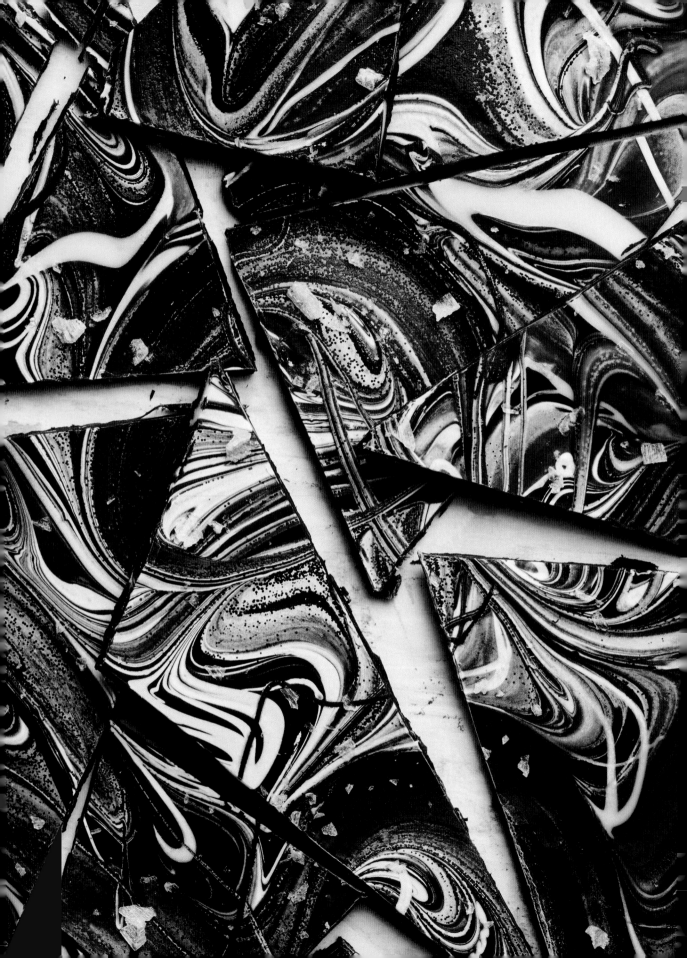

This bark looks formal with its intermingled swirls of dark and white chocolate. But despite its dressed-up appearance, the bark is easy to make. Whether you present it on a plate or package it up as a gift, it's sure to draw attention — and compliments.

TUXEDO CHOCOLATE BARK

12 ounces (340 g) good-quality 70% bittersweet (dark) chocolate, chopped into ¼-inch (0.5 cm) pieces, divided

•

12 ounces (340 g) good-quality white chocolate, chopped into ¼-inch (0.5 cm) pieces, divided

•

Flaky sea salt

RIMMED BAKING SHEET, LINED WITH PARCHMENT PAPER

1 Set aside ½ cup (125 mL) dark chocolate and ½ cup (125 mL) white chocolate in separate small bowls.

2 In a medium microwave-safe bowl, microwave the remaining dark chocolate on High in 30-second intervals, stirring in between, until melted. (Alternatively, melt it on the stove; see page 15 for details.) Immediately add the reserved dark chocolate and stir until melted and shiny.

3 In a separate medium microwave-safe bowl, microwave the remaining white chocolate on High in 15-second intervals, stirring in between, until melted — it will melt faster than the dark chocolate. (Alternatively, melt it on the stove.) Immediately add the reserved white chocolate and stir until melted and shiny.

4 Pour the dark chocolate onto the prepared baking sheet. Pour the white chocolate over the dark in a zigzag pattern from side to side. Draw a spatula through the chocolate, zigzagging from top to bottom, to create dramatic swirls. Quickly sprinkle with flakes of salt.

5 Let the bark set at room temperature for at least 1 hour or overnight. If the room is warm, transfer it to the refrigerator for 10 minutes. The bark is set if you can lift out the parchment liner and the chocolate doesn't sag in the middle. Once the chocolate has set, break it into pieces.

TIPS

See page 15 for tips on buying and chopping chocolate for melting.

Store the bark in an airtight container in a cool place for up to 2 weeks.

These red, white and green treats add a festive touch to the goodie tray without needing food coloring. Since the clusters are freeform and meant to be a bit lumpy, they are ideal for kids who are eager to help with holiday baking. Santa (or his helpers) will be pleased to find some beside the milk on Christmas Eve.

CHRISTMAS CLUSTERS

1/4 cup (40 g)
roasted pistachios,
divided

•

1/4 cup (40 g)
dried cranberries,
divided

•

8 ounces (225 g)
white chocolate, chopped

BAKING SHEET, LINED WITH PARCHMENT PAPER

1 Set aside 12 pistachios and 12 cranberries in separate small bowls for the garnish.

2 Chop the remaining pistachios and cranberries separately.

3 In a medium microwave-safe bowl, heat the white chocolate on High in 15-second intervals, stirring in between. (Alternatively, melt it on the stove; see page 15 for details.) Once the chocolate is melted and smooth, stir in the chopped pistachios and cranberries.

4 Using a spoon, drop the mixture onto the prepared baking sheet, creating 12 clusters spaced apart. Top each with a reserved pistachio and cranberry.

5 Let cool completely at room temperature.

TIPS

White chocolate picks up flavors quickly. Be sure the clusters are not stored with other goodies, or their flavors might transfer.

Store the clusters in an airtight container in a cool place for up to 2 weeks.

This casual recipe takes its inspiration from fondue (and a bit of laziness). Instead of dipping the strawberries ahead of time, I have my guests sweep a berry through melted chocolate, scooping up as much or as little as they like. It's also a fun way to find out who likes white chocolate and who likes dark.

CHOCOLATE-DIPPED STRAWBERRIES

12 large fresh strawberries (see Tips)

●

6 ounces (175 g) good-quality 70% bittersweet (dark) chocolate, chopped

●

6 ounces (175 g) good-quality white chocolate, chopped

12 BAMBOO SKEWERS

1 Pierce each strawberry through the hull with a bamboo skewer, about three-quarters of the way through. (You want the strawberry to stay on the end of the skewer, so don't pierce it all the way through.) Set aside.

2 In a medium microwave-safe bowl, heat the dark chocolate in the microwave on High in 30-second intervals, stirring in between, until melted. (Alternatively, melt it on the stove; see page 15 for details.) Set aside.

3 In a medium microwave-safe bowl, heat the white chocolate in the microwave on High in 15-second intervals, stirring in between, until melted — it will melt faster than the dark chocolate. (Alternatively, melt it on the stove.)

4 As soon as the white chocolate is melted, pour the dark chocolate onto a plate. Immediately pour the white chocolate over the dark chocolate in a zigzag pattern.

5 Place the melted chocolate and strawberries on the table so guests can roll the skewered berries through the chocolate, picking up a bit of both dark and white. Eat immediately.

TIPS

Make sure the strawberries are completely dry when you serve them.
Any water on them will seize the chocolate.

The strawberries taste best the day they are made. If you need to
refrigerate dipped strawberries, let them harden on parchment paper,
then place them in an airtight container lined with a clean paper towel.
Dipped strawberries will keep for up to 2 days.

My father isn't a chocolate fan . . . but combine it with raspberries? He'll take it in pies, cakes, cookies, ice cream or its purest form: chocolate-filled raspberries. Sure, the berries are small and filling them takes a few minutes, but the results are worth it. Having downed a few (dozen) during the testing phase, I'm now convinced the tiny raspberry was designed for a chocolate filling. Do your own research and see if you agree.

CHOCOLATE-FILLED RASPBERRIES

1 ounce (30 g)
70% bittersweet (dark)
chocolate, chopped

•

1 teaspoon (5 mL)
heavy or whipping
(35%) cream

•

1 cup (125 g)
fresh raspberries

RESEALABLE PLASTIC BAG

MINI MUFFIN PAN

1 In a small microwave-safe bowl, combine the dark chocolate and cream. Heat in the microwave on High in 15-second intervals, stirring in between, until melted. (Alternatively, melt it on the stove; see page 15 for details.) Let cool to room temperature.

2 Pour the melted chocolate into a resealable plastic bag. Cut a tiny hole in one corner. Place the cut corner inside a raspberry and gently squeeze until the berry is full. Place the filled raspberry in one well of a mini muffin pan to keep it upright (you should be able to fit a couple of berries in each well, depending on their size). Repeat with the remaining raspberries and chocolate. Transfer to the refrigerator until the chocolate has set, about 20 minutes.

TIPS

If you don't have a mini muffin pan, use a regular muffin pan.
Place as many raspberries as you can in each well, open side up,
making sure you don't squeeze them so tightly they break.
The raspberries will hold each other upright while you fill them.

Leftover raspberries can be refrigerated in an airtight container for up to 2 days.

Water and chocolate have an odd relationship. A drop of water can seize melting chocolate, making it granular and lumpy, but add a lot of water and chocolate becomes silky and cooperative. Dairy-free, egg-free chocolate mousse was originally developed by Hervé This, a French chemist and pioneer of molecular gastronomy. I've adapted his technique and added a pinch of chipotle, because I like to complicate things. Chipotle not your thing? Omit it. Like a fancy topping? Try Chantilly Cream (page 206). No matter how you choose to make it, be prepared to be amazed. Nothing so simple should taste so good.

SPICED DAIRY-FREE CHOCOLATE MOUSSE

1 tablespoon (15 mL) salt

•

8 ounces (225 g) good-quality 70% bittersweet (dark) chocolate, chopped

•

1/8 teaspoon (0.5 mL) chipotle powder

RIMMED BAKING SHEET, LINED WITH A TEA TOWEL

FOUR 1/2-CUP (125 mL) RAMEKINS OR SMALL DESSERT BOWLS

1 Fill a large bowl halfway with ice and water. Add the salt and stir to combine. Set aside.

2 In a medium saucepan, heat 3/4 cup (175 mL) water, the chocolate and the chipotle powder over medium-low heat, whisking constantly until smooth.

3 Pour the chocolate mixture into a medium heatproof bowl. Place the ice-water bowl on the prepared baking sheet. Place the bowl of chocolate in the water bath. Whisk the chocolate until thickened, about 5 minutes. Stop when you see strands of chocolate forming inside the loops of the whisk — if you over-whisk, it will become granular (see Tips).

4 Working quickly, spoon the mousse into ramekins. Serve immediately or cover and refrigerate for up to 3 days.

TIPS

If the mixture becomes granular, return the chocolate to the saucepan and remelt it, then return it to the bowl in the ice bath and whisk again. Since there is no dairy in this recipe, the remelting and whisking process can be repeated multiple times, if needed — but you'll nail it quickly.

Instead of using plain water in Step 2, try this with coffee, for a mocha mousse.

When a dessert shows up on restaurant menus, people assume it's hard to make and time-consuming and requires exotic ingredients. This entertaining-worthy dessert is none of those things. It's easy to make, comes together in minutes and uses ingredients you can find in any grocery store. Spoon it into your best dishes, then bask in the praise.

QUICK CHOCOLATE MOUSSE

10 ounces (300 g) bittersweet (dark) chocolate chips, divided

•

2 cups (500 mL) cold heavy or whipping (35%) cream

•

¼ cup (35 g) confectioners' (icing) sugar

ELECTRIC MIXER

1 Finely chop 1 tablespoon (15 mL) chocolate chips. Set aside.

2 Meanwhile, in a medium microwave-safe bowl, heat the remaining chocolate chips in the microwave on High in 30-second intervals, stirring in between, until about three-quarters have melted. Stir gently until all the chips have melted. (Alternatively, melt them on the stove; see page 15 for details.) Set aside to cool to room temperature, about 10 minutes.

3 Meanwhile, in a large bowl, using an electric mixer on high speed, whip together the cream and confectioners' sugar until stiff peaks form. Refrigerate the whipped cream until the chocolate has cooled.

4 Set aside about ½ cup (125 mL) whipped cream. Pour the cooled chocolate over the remaining whipped cream and, using the mixer, whip until just combined, about 30 seconds.

5 Evenly spoon the mousse into ramekins, wineglasses or small bowls. Top with the reserved whipped cream and sprinkle with the chopped chocolate. Serve immediately.

TIPS

If you don't have an electric mixer, you can use a whisk to whip the cream by hand. This will take a lot longer but will produce the same results, and will burn a few extra calories!

The mousse, prepared through Step 5 (without the reserved topping), can be covered and refrigerated for up to 3 days.

This is the ultimate in decadence. It's like a silky chocolate truffle but in sliceable form. People will think you slaved for hours, when really the only trick to this recipe is planning ahead to ensure it has enough time to chill. If anyone asks, tell them it took you hours to create — which is technically true. After all, waiting is hard work when chocolate is involved.

CHOCOLATE PÂTÉ

6 ounces (175 g) good-quality 70% bittersweet (dark) chocolate, chopped

•

1 1/3 cups (325 mL) heavy or whipping (35%) cream, divided

•

1/4 cup (60 g) salted butter, softened

5 3/4- BY 3-INCH (14 BY 7.5 CM) MINI LOAF PAN, LINED WITH PLASTIC WRAP WITH A 2-INCH (5 CM) OVERHANG

ELECTRIC MIXER (OPTIONAL)

1 Place the chocolate, 2/3 cup (150 mL) cream and the butter in a medium microwave-safe bowl. Heat in the microwave on High in 30-second intervals, stirring in between, until melted and smooth. (Alternatively, use a medium saucepan over low heat, stirring occasionally until smooth.)

2 Spread the chocolate evenly in the prepared pan. Cover with plastic wrap and refrigerate until firm enough to slice, at least 6 hours, or up to 3 days.

3 Thirty minutes before serving, remove the pâté from the refrigerator and let it stand at room temperature.

4 Meanwhile, place the remaining cream in a small bowl and chill in the freezer for 10 minutes. Using a whisk or electric mixer, whip it until stiff peaks form.

5 Remove the pâté from the pan (using the plastic-wrap liner) and slice it into 8 pieces. Place 2 pieces on a plate and top with a dollop of whipped cream. Serve immediately. Return any leftover pâté to the refrigerator immediately.

TIP

If you don't have a small loaf pan or similar container for the pâté, use a muffin pan instead. Line 4 wells of a standard muffin pan with parchment or foil-lined papers. Spoon in equal amounts of the chocolate, smooth it flat and chill, creating individual portions. Top with a dollop of whipped cream, of course.

I have a confession to make: I don't really like white chocolate. At least, I didn't until I was introduced to it in caramelized form, which tastes a bit like dulce de leche and a bit like toffee but has a unique quality all its own. While you can find caramelized white chocolate in some specialty shops, you can easily make it yourself. It just takes a bit of time and patience.

CARAMELIZED WHITE CHOCOLATE TRUFFLES

12 ounces (340 g) good-quality white chocolate, finely chopped

•

1/2 cup (125 mL) heavy or whipping (35%) cream

•

1 pound (455 g) good-quality bittersweet (dark) chocolate, chopped

PREHEAT THE OVEN TO 250°F (120°C)

8-INCH (20 CM) SQUARE GLASS BAKING DISH

2 BAKING SHEETS, LINED WITH PARCHMENT PAPER

RESEALABLE PLASTIC BAG

1 Sprinkle the white chocolate into the baking dish in a shallow layer. Bake in the preheated oven, stirring every 10 minutes, until the chocolate is a dark golden amber and smooth, about 60 to 90 minutes. Partway through the process it will turn grainy, but don't panic — the chocolate will loosen up again as it caramelizes. (For more information on caramelizing white chocolate, see page 15.)

2 Set aside 1/4 cup (60 mL) of the caramelized white chocolate in a small microwave-safe bowl, for drizzling. Scrape the remaining caramelized chocolate into a medium heatproof bowl.

3 In a small saucepan over medium heat, warm the cream until it starts to simmer and small bubbles form around the edges of the pan. Pour the hot cream and a generous pinch of salt over the caramelized chocolate; stir until shiny and smooth. Refrigerate until the mixture cools to room temperature.

4 Scoop up 1 tablespoon (15 mL) of the mixture at a time and form into balls. Place on a prepared baking sheet. Freeze until firm, about 15 minutes.

5 In a deep medium microwave-safe bowl, heat the dark chocolate in the microwave on High in 30-second intervals, stirring in between, until about three-quarters has melted. Stir gently until all the chocolate has melted. (Alternatively, melt it on the stove; see page 15 for details.)

6 Place a truffle on a fork and quickly submerge it in the melted chocolate. Hold the dipped truffle over the bowl for a few seconds and gently tap the hand holding the fork to help excess chocolate drip off. Place the truffle on the second prepared baking sheet. Continue dipping, one truffle at a time, until all are coated. Refrigerate for 10 minutes so the coating will harden.

7 Heat the reserved caramelized white chocolate in the microwave on High in 15-second intervals, stirring in between, until melted. Transfer to a small resealable plastic bag.

8 Cut a tiny piece from one corner of the bag. Squeeze the bag gently as you move back and forth over the dipped truffles to form zigzag patterns. Return the truffles to the refrigerator to harden.

TIP

Store the truffles in an airtight container in the refrigerator for up to 2 weeks. Truffles taste best at room temperature.

My husband and I didn't have a wedding cake. Instead we had a tower of assorted homemade truffles, and my favorite is hazelnut. This simplified version skips the chocolate coating in favor of finely ground hazelnuts. So far no one has complained about this omission — perhaps because I tell them the calories they're saving allow for a second truffle.

HAZELNUT TRUFFLES

8 ounces (225 g) good-quality 70% bittersweet (dark) chocolate, chopped

•

2 cups (300 g) toasted hazelnuts, ground (see Tips), divided

•

1 cup (250 mL) heavy or whipping (35%) cream

BAKING SHEET, LINED WITH PARCHMENT PAPER

1 In a medium bowl, combine the chocolate and $\frac{1}{2}$ cup (75 g) ground hazelnuts.

2 In a small saucepan over medium heat, heat the cream until bubbles form around the edges of the pan. Immediately pour the hot cream over the chocolate mixture and stir until the chocolate is melted. Cover and refrigerate until cold and thick, about 1 hour.

3 Remove from the refrigerator and whisk the mixture until light and creamy, about 30 seconds. Do not overbeat, or the mixture could separate. Scoop up 1 tablespoon (15 mL) at a time and form into balls (see Tips). Place on the prepared baking sheet. Refrigerate until firm, about 30 minutes.

4 Spread the remaining ground hazelnuts on a plate. Remove the truffles from the refrigerator and, working quickly, roll each in the ground nuts to coat.

TIPS

To toast hazelnuts, place the shelled nuts on a rimmed baking sheet and toast in an oven preheated to 350°F (180°C), until fragrant, about 10 minutes. Transfer the hot nuts to a towel and rub to remove as much of the skins as possible. Let the hazelnuts cool, then grind in a food processor or blender until very finely chopped.

The truffles don't have to be perfect spheres. Smooth any obvious peaks by rolling the truffles with your fingertips — not your palms, which might be too warm and could melt the chocolate.

Store the truffles in an airtight container in the refrigerator for up to 1 week.

FRUIT

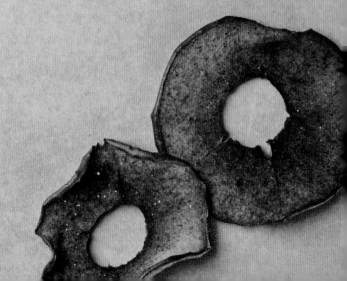

Turns out fruit leather isn't just for kids. My test batches disappeared thanks to the 40+ crowd. I even found myself wandering into the kitchen for "just one more strip." Will kids like it? I hope not. The adults around here don't want to share.

STRAWBERRY ROLL-UPS

4 cups (560 g)
sliced hulled strawberries

•

1 tablespoon (15 mL)
freshly squeezed
lemon juice

•

1 tablespoon (15 mL)
honey

PREHEAT THE OVEN TO ITS LOWEST SETTING, 150°F TO 170°F (70°C TO 80°C)

BLENDER

2 RIMMED BAKING SHEETS, LINED WITH PARCHMENT PAPER

1 Place the strawberries, lemon juice and honey in a blender. Blend on high speed until smooth.

2 Pour the fruit mixture onto the prepared baking sheets to form a layer between 1/8 inch (3 mm) and 1/4 inch (0.5 cm) thick. Spread with a spatula if the mixture doesn't look even. Resist the temptation to make the layer thicker than 1/4 inch (0.5 cm), or the leather will crack and not dry out properly. (See Tips for what to do with any excess.)

3 Bake in the preheated oven, with the racks placed in the upper and lower thirds of the oven, until the mixture is dry yet pliable, about 4 to 6 hours, depending on thickness and oven temperature.

4 Remove from the oven and place a fresh sheet of parchment paper over the fruit leather. Press to adhere. Flip onto a flat work surface so the fresh parchment is on the bottom. Peel away the layer of parchment that the leather was baked on. Using scissors or a pizza cutter, remove any uneven edges, then cut into strips 2 inches (5 cm) wide. Roll up the strips. Eat immediately or at room temperature.

TIPS

Any excess fruit mixture can be used in a smoothie or poured over Vanilla Ice Cream (page 184).

Store the roll-ups at room temperature in an airtight container for up to 2 weeks.

This recipe is a bit of a showstopper. Little wonder — it's hard to compete with flames. While the warm pineapple is delicious on its own, it's the perfect pairing for cool desserts with Vanilla Ice Cream (page 184) or Chantilly Cream (page 206).

FLAMING PINEAPPLE

½ cup (110 g) Cinnamon
Sugar (page 20)

•

1 can (14 oz/398 mL)
pineapple slices (8 rings),
drained and patted dry

•

1 tablespoon (15 mL)
rum

LARGE, HEAVY-BOTTOMED SKILLET

BARBECUE LIGHTER OR LONG MATCH

1 Place the cinnamon sugar in a shallow bowl. One at a time, press the pineapple rings into the sugar, coating both sides.

2 Heat a large, heavy skillet over medium heat. Add the pineapple rings in a single layer. Cook until browned, about 2 minutes. Flip the rings and cook on the other side until browned, about 2 more minutes. Turn off the heat.

3 In a small microwave-safe mug, heat the rum in the microwave on High until just warm, about 10 seconds.

4 Pour the warmed rum over the pineapple. Using a barbecue lighter or long match, light the rum. The initial flames can leap up, so make sure your hand and clothes are out of the way. (See Tips if you've never intentionally set fire to your food before.) Once the alcohol has burned off, let stand for a minute or two.

5 Transfer the warm pineapple slices to serving plates and drizzle with sauce from the pan.

TIPS

You can use 8 fresh pineapple rings (if available) that are about ½ inch (1 cm) thick. Increase the cooking time to about 4 minutes per side.

If your pan is too small to hold all the rings in a single layer, cook and flambé them in two batches.

If you've never flambéed before, you can do a quick practice run before guests arrive. Pour 1 tablespoon (15 mL) warm rum into the empty skillet and light it as in Step 4. When you're ready to make the dessert, you'll now have a good idea of how much the rum will flare up.

Any leftovers can be stored in an airtight container in the refrigerator for up to 3 days.

These strawberries straddle the fence between a standalone dessert and a sauce.
They can be eaten warm from the oven or cold from the fridge, drizzled over ice
cream, stirred into yogurt or even spooned over Buttermilk Scones (page 88).
I've no idea how you'll enjoy them, but I do know you will enjoy them.

BALSAMIC ROASTED STRAWBERRIES

2 cups (280 g)
sliced hulled fresh
strawberries (see Tips)

•

1 tablespoon (15 mL)
good-quality balsamic
vinegar

•

2 tablespoons (30 g)
Vanilla Sugar (page 22)

PREHEAT THE OVEN TO 425°F (220°C)

RIMMED BAKING SHEET, LINED WITH PARCHMENT PAPER

1 In a medium bowl, toss the strawberries with the balsamic vinegar.

2 Spread the berries in a single layer on the prepared baking sheet. Sprinkle evenly with the vanilla sugar.

3 Bake on the middle rack of the preheated oven for 10 to 15 minutes or until the sugar bubbles and the berries are tender. Let cool slightly for 10 minutes, then transfer the berries and juice to serving bowls.

TIPS

When slicing the strawberries, try to cut the pieces to the same size for even baking. To do this, take your cue from the smallest berries. Halve the smallest ones to determine your base size, then cut the bigger berries to match.

Be sure to use a good-quality balsamic vinegar. Not sure if the balsamic in your cupboard will do? Take a sip to test it. If the vinegar makes you pucker, save it for salad dressings and splurge on a small bottle of quality balsamic for desserts like this one.

Like this recipe? Double (or triple) the ingredients. But make sure the berries are roasted in a single layer, which might mean you will need a second pan.

The roasted strawberries can be stored in an airtight container in the refrigerator for up to 3 days.

Good things come in twos. Like this recipe: two apples, two hundred degrees and two hours. Too good to be true? No. These chips work every time.

CRISPY APPLE RINGS

2 tablespoons (30 g)
Cinnamon Sugar
(page 20), approx.

•

¼ teaspoon (1 mL)
ground ginger

•

2 large apples,
cored and sliced into
¹/₁₆-inch (2 mm) rings

PREHEAT THE OVEN TO 200°F (100°C)

2 BAKING SHEETS, LINED WITH PARCHMENT PAPER

1 In a small bowl, combine the cinnamon sugar and ginger.

2 Place the apple slices flat in a single layer on the prepared baking sheets, ensuring that they don't touch. Sprinkle lightly with the sugar mixture (depending on the size of your apples, you might not need all the sugar).

3 Bake in the preheated oven, with the racks placed in the upper and lower thirds of the oven, until the apple slices feel leathery, about 2 hours.

4 Turn off the oven and stick a wooden spoon handle in the door opening to keep it ajar. Let the rings cool completely in the oven. They will become crisp as they cool.

TIPS

This recipe works with any apple variety you care to use.
The more thinly you slice the apples, the crisper the rings will be.

Store the apple rings at room temperature in either a lidded glass jar or a resealable plastic bag with the air pressed out for up to 1 week.

Starting with almond flour (sometimes called almond meal or ground almonds)
instead of whole nuts helps these bars come together quickly. That's the good news.
The bad news? They're so tasty you might have to make them pretty often.

FRUIT BARS

1 cup (110 g)
almond flour

•

1 cup (160 g)
mixed dried fruit (I use
blueberries, cherries
and cranberries)

•

1/2 cup (80 g)
roughly chopped pitted
dates

FOOD PROCESSOR OR BLENDER

9- BY 5-INCH (23 BY 12.5 CM) METAL LOAF PAN, LINED WITH PARCHMENT PAPER

1 In a food processor or blender, combine the almond flour, dried fruit, dates and a pinch of salt. Pulse in 5-second intervals, scraping down the sides of the container as necessary, until the mixture becomes pliable. Gradually increase the interval time until you can process continuously and the mixture forms a ball (the timing will depend on the strength of the machine).

2 Scrape the mixture into the prepared pan and press it flat.

3 Place plastic wrap directly on the surface and refrigerate until set, at least 1 hour or overnight. Remove from the pan, using the parchment liner. Remove the plastic wrap, then cut into bars. Eat cold or at room temperature.

TIP

Store the bars in an airtight container in the refrigerator for up to 2 weeks.

I'm that person — I shake and rattle and cajole a bag of jellies until the flavor
I want gets shuffled to the top. In the end I'm left with a jumble of unwelcome
black and yellow candies, which I "generously" share with friends and family. But
this recipe changes the game. It allows me total control over the flavors, but it also
means I have to share my favorites. No worries. It's easy to make more.

FRUIT JELLIES

2 packets
(each ¼ oz/7 g)
unflavored gelatin

•

⅓ cup (75 mL)
fruit juice, such as
grape, cranberry or
orange-mango (see Tips)

•

¼ cup (55 g)
granulated sugar

SILICONE ICE-CUBE TRAY OR MOLDS

1 Place 2 tablespoons (30 mL) water in a small bowl and sprinkle with the gelatin. Let stand for 5 minutes to soften.

2 In a small saucepan over medium heat, heat together the juice and sugar, stirring occasionally, until the sugar is dissolved, about 3 minutes. Remove from the heat and stir in the softened gelatin until dissolved.

3 Pour the mixture into 12 wells of a silicone ice-cube tray or molds. Refrigerate until firm, about 1 hour, or overnight.

4 To unmold the jellies, twist the silicone and use the edge of a knife or your finger to gently pry the jellies from the molds.

TIPS

Fresh tropical fruit juices — such as papaya, kiwi, mango, guava and pineapple — contain an enzyme called bromelain that prevents gelatin from setting. If you want to make jellies with these flavors, use processed (not fresh) juices, as pasteurization destroys the enzyme.

While you can make jellies with any fruit juice, clear juices such as apple (not cider), grape and cranberry will deliver more luminous results.

If you don't have silicone molds, use an 8- by 4-inch (20 by 10 cm) loaf pan lined with foil and lightly greased. Once the jelly has set (about 90 minutes), turn it out onto a clean work surface and cut with a sharp knife into 12 cubes.

The jellies will keep in an airtight container in the refrigerator for up to 1 week.

Don't let these little pots fool you. They may be small, but they're filling. They're also silky smooth, gently tangy and utterly decadent.

LEMON POTS

2 lemons

•

2¹/₂ cups (625 mL) heavy or whipping (35%) cream, divided

•

²/₃ cup (150 g) granulated sugar

SIX ¹/₂-CUP (125 ML) RAMEKINS, GLASSES OR MASON JARS

ELECTRIC MIXER

1 Grate the zest from the lemons and juice them, making 2 tablespoons (30 mL) zest and ¹/₂ cup (125 mL) juice. (Reserve any extra for another use; see page 16 for details).

2 In a small saucepan, whisk together 2 cups (500 mL) cream, the sugar, 1 tablespoon (15 mL) lemon zest and the lemon juice. Bring to a boil over medium heat, then reduce to a simmer and cook for 3 minutes, stirring constantly. Remove from the heat and let cool for 15 minutes.

3 Pour equal quantities of the mixture into each ramekin. Cover and refrigerate until set, at least 6 hours, or overnight. Set aside the remaining 1 tablespoon (15 mL) lemon zest in an airtight container for garnishing later.

4 In a small bowl, using an electric mixer on high speed, whip the remaining cream until stiff peaks form. Top the lemon pots with a dollop of whipped cream and a sprinkle of lemon zest before serving.

TIP

Leftover lemon pots (without the whipped cream topping) can be covered and stored in the refrigerator for up to 5 days.

I first heard about roasting fruit with white chocolate from a Scandinavian chef. As a stalwart fan of dark chocolate, I was skeptical, but she assured me this combination would change my mind. It did.

ROASTED MIXED BERRIES WITH WHITE CHOCOLATE

4 cups (1 L)
mixed fresh berries
(any combination of
raspberries, blackberries,
blueberries and/or
sliced strawberries)

•

4 ounces (115 g)
white chocolate,
finely chopped

•

1 tablespoon (15 mL)
grated lime zest

PREHEAT THE OVEN TO 425°F (220°C)

RIMMED BAKING SHEET, LINED WITH PARCHMENT PAPER

1 Spread the fruit in a single layer on the prepared baking sheet. Sprinkle evenly with the white chocolate and lime zest.

2 Bake on the middle rack of the preheated oven until the chocolate has melted and the fruit is hot but not softened, about 5 to 8 minutes.

3 Immediately spoon into bowls. Eat warm.

TIP

Leftovers can be stored in an airtight container in the refrigerator for up to 3 days. Reheat in the microwave on High in 15-second intervals, stirring in between, until the chocolate is beginning to melt.

Every summer my mom used to make small batches of pear and ginger jam, using local fruit. To stretch the limited supply, she would use the smallest jars possible, bringing them out at regular intervals only after the snow arrived. The combination of summer pears and warm ginger served as an antidote to the cold, dark winter. This crisp pays homage to Mom's favorite combination. Like her jam, there's never any left. Unlike her jam, I can make this any time of year.

GINGERY PEAR CRISP

3 cans (each 14 oz/ 398 mL) pear halves packed in fruit juice

•

1 tablespoon (15 g) minced crystalized ginger

•

1 cup (120 g) crushed gingersnap cookies (about 16)

PREHEAT THE OVEN TO 350°F (180°C)

9- BY 5-INCH (23 BY 12.5 CM) GLASS OR CERAMIC LOAF DISH, BUTTERED

1 Drain the pears, reserving ¼ cup (60 mL) juice. (See Tips for using leftover juice.)

2 Chop the pears into ½-inch (1 cm) pieces and place in the prepared dish. Add the reserved juice and crystalized ginger, tossing to coat the pears.

3 Sprinkle the crushed gingersnap cookies evenly over the pears.

4 Bake on the middle rack of the preheated oven until the pears are bubbling, about 20 to 25 minutes. Serve warm.

TIPS

Don't toss the remaining pear juice. Add it to fruit smoothies or mix with sparkling water for a refreshing spritzer.

This dish can also be made with canned peaches or with a combination of peaches and pears.

Leftover crisp (if there is any) can be covered and refrigerated overnight. Enjoy cold the next day or reheat for 10 minutes in an oven preheated to 250°F (120°C).

Baked fruit comes in many forms. While the differences between a crisp, a crumble and a betty aren't well defined, the cobbler stands alone. It's named for its signature lumpy quick-bread topping, which resembles rough cobblestones (this might come in handy on trivia night). Either way, this cobbler goes well with a scoop of Salted Caramel Ice Cream (page 187) or Buttered Rum Sauce (page 210).

PEACH COBBLER

2 cans (each 28 oz/796 mL) peach slices in light syrup (with liquid)

•

2 cups (280 g) self-rising flour (page 19)

•

½ cup (115 g) cold salted butter

PREHEAT THE OVEN TO 350°F (180°C)

8-INCH (20 CM) SQUARE GLASS BAKING DISH, BUTTERED

1 Remove the peaches from the cans, reserving the syrup from 1 can (about 14 tablespoons/200 mL). Chop the fruit into ½-inch (1 cm) pieces. Place the peach pieces in the prepared dish.

2 Place the flour in a medium bowl. Using the large holes of a box grater, grate the cold butter over the flour. Toss to coat the butter and distribute it evenly throughout. Pour the reserved peach syrup over the flour and stir to combine. Spoon the batter over the peaches in 6 equal dollops.

3 Bake in the middle of the preheated oven until the peaches are bubbling and a tester inserted into the topping comes out clean, about 45 minutes.

4 Let cool on a wire rack until cool enough to eat but still warm, about 30 minutes to 1 hour. Serve warm.

TIPS

Leftover peach syrup can be added to smoothies or used to sweeten fruit punch. If you can't use it right away, freeze it in ice-cube trays, then transfer to a resealable freezer bag for later use.

This recipe can easily be doubled and baked in a 13- by 9-inch (33 by 23 cm) glass baking dish for 60 to 75 minutes.

Any leftover cobbler can be covered and refrigerated for up to 3 days. Enjoy cold or warm in an oven preheated to 250°F (120°C) for 10 to 15 minutes.

CREAMY THINGS

I first tried this dessert more than 20 years ago while in Portugal. My friend Joe was acting as tour guide and recommended it, promoting it as a classic local dish. In a typical Joe move, he waited until after I'd placed my order to casually mention that the name translates to "camel spit." I've no idea how it ended up with such an inelegant name, but this light, decadent dulce de leche mousse deserves better PR.

BABA DE CAMELO

²/₃ cup (150 mL)
dulce de leche (see Tips)

•

3 large eggs,
separated and brought
to room temperature

•

¹/₄ cup (30 g)
almond slices

ELECTRIC MIXER

FOUR ¹/₂-CUP (125 ML) RAMEKINS OR SMALL DESSERT BOWLS

1 In a large bowl, whisk together the dulce de leche and egg yolks until smooth.

2 In another large bowl, using an electric mixer on high speed, beat the egg whites until stiff peaks form. Fold one-third of the whites into the dulce de leche mixture. Then gently fold in the remaining whites.

3 Spoon the mixture into ramekins, cover and refrigerate until firm, at least 6 hours, or overnight.

4 Right before serving, add the almonds to a nonstick skillet over medium-low heat. Toast, stirring every 30 seconds or so, until the nuts become fragrant and are just beginning to turn golden brown. Their natural oils will continue to cook them for a minute or two once removed from the heat, so take them off sooner than you think you should. Spread on a plate and let cool slightly, then sprinkle on the chilled dessert right before serving.

TIPS

Dulce de leche can be found in well-stocked grocery stores, but its location can vary. Sometimes it's shelved with jams and spreads, sometimes it's in the Latin section, and sometimes it's with the sweetened condensed milk.

This recipe contains raw eggs. If you are concerned about the safety of raw eggs, you can substitute eggs pasteurized in the shell.

This recipe can be made ahead of time. If using pasteurized eggs, consume it within 3 days. If using unpasteurized eggs, consume within 24 hours.

No one knows where the term "fool" comes from. I've a few ideas: You'd be a fool to pass on this dessert. It's so simple even a fool can make it. Or, most likely — at least in our house — certain unnamed people try to fool each other into thinking it's all gone by hiding the leftovers behind big bags of salad.

RASPBERRY FOOL

2 cups (280 g)
raspberries, thawed
if frozen, divided

•

1/4 cup (55 g)
Vanilla Sugar (page 22),
divided

•

1 1/2 cups (375 mL)
cold heavy or whipping
(35%) cream

ELECTRIC MIXER

1 Set aside 1/2 cup (70 g) raspberries.

2 In a medium bowl, using the tines of a fork, gently crush the remaining raspberries and sprinkle with 2 tablespoons (30 g) vanilla sugar. Let stand for 10 minutes.

3 In another medium bowl, using an electric mixer on high speed, whip the cream with the remaining vanilla sugar until stiff peaks form.

4 Fold the crushed raspberries into the whipped cream, leaving some swirled through for effect.

5 Spoon into dishes and top with the remaining berries. Serve immediately.

TIP

Leftover fool can be covered and stored in the refrigerator for up to 2 days.

This mousse draws inspiration from classic Vietnamese iced coffee, which is cold strong coffee combined with sweetened condensed milk. While I wouldn't promote this as a breakfast food, it is a delicious way to end the evening meal.

COFFEE MOUSSE

1 can (14 oz or 300 mL)
full-fat sweetened
condensed milk

•

1 tablespoon (15 mL)
instant espresso powder,
plus 1 teaspoon (5 mL)
for garnish (optional)

•

2 cups (500 mL)
cold heavy or whipping
(35%) cream

ELECTRIC MIXER

SIX ¾-CUP (175 ML) RAMEKINS OR DESSERT BOWLS

FINE-MESH SIEVE

1 In a large bowl, combine the condensed milk and espresso powder. Cover and refrigerate until cold, about 1 hour.

2 Give the coffee mixture a stir. Pour the cold cream over the coffee mixture. Using an electric mixer on low speed, mix together until combined. Increase the speed to high and beat until soft peaks form, about 10 minutes.

3 Spoon the mixture into ramekins or bowls. Using a fine-mesh sieve, dust the tops lightly with more espresso powder, if desired. Cover and refrigerate until the mousse is cold and firm, about 4 hours, or overnight.

TIPS

Instant espresso powder can be found in well-stocked grocery stores.

Mousse not your style? Can I tempt you with coffee ice cream?
Skip the espresso powder garnish and just spoon the whipped mixture into a freezer-safe airtight container. Freeze for at least 6 hours or up to 2 weeks.

The mousse can be covered and refrigerated for up to 2 days.

If there were an award for best non-traditional holiday dessert, my mom's friend Lyn would win the prize. This is her signature recipe: a creamy dessert you'd never guess is frozen. She brought it every year to Mom's Christmas party, and even though the table was laden with goodies of all flavors, shapes and kinds, I ignored them to save room for a helping (or two) of her maple panna cotta — and I have no regrets.

MAPLE PANNA COTTA POTS

1 envelope
(2$\frac{1}{2}$ teaspoons/7 g)
unflavored gelatin

•

*2 cups (500 mL)
pure maple syrup,
divided*

•

*3 cups (750 mL) cold
heavy or whipping (35%)
cream, divided*

ELECTRIC MIXER

EIGHT $^3/_4$-CUP (175 ML) RAMEKINS OR SMALL BOWLS, LIGHTLY BUTTERED

1 In a medium heatproof bowl, combine the gelatin and 1 tablespoon (15 mL) water. Set aside.

2 In a small pot over medium heat, bring 1$\frac{1}{2}$ cups (375 mL) maple syrup to a boil, about 5 minutes, stirring occasionally. Immediately pour the hot maple syrup over the softened gelatin. Stir well until the gelatin is completely dissolved, about 1 to 2 minutes. Set aside to cool until no longer hot to the touch, about 30 minutes. Place plastic wrap directly on the surface and refrigerate until it's cold and has the consistency of pudding, about 60 to 90 minutes.

3 In a large bowl, using an electric mixer on high speed, whip 2 cups (500 mL) cold cream until stiff peaks form. Gently fold the maple jelly into the whipped cream (see Tip). Spoon the mixture into the prepared ramekins and smooth the tops. Cover with plastic wrap and freeze for at least 2 hours or overnight.

4 Just before serving, in a medium bowl, using an electric mixer on high speed, whip the remaining cream until stiff peaks form.

5 Serve each pot topped with a dollop of whipped cream and a generous drizzle (about 1 tablespoon/15 mL) of maple syrup. Immediately return any leftovers to the freezer and store for up to 1 week.

TIP

If the maple gelatin mixture sets firmly before you can add it to the whipped cream, you will need to soften it slightly first. Transfer the gelatin mixture to a medium microwave-safe bowl and microwave on High in 15-second intervals, stirring in between, until loose enough to stir into the whipped cream but not warm.

My husband knows me so well. If a restaurant has crème brûlée on the menu, he'll tell me to save room for dessert. While I can pass up crème caramel without blinking, I have no willpower when it comes to this silky, hard-topped creation.

CRÈME BRÛLÉE

1½ cups (375 mL)
*heavy or whipping
(35%) cream*

•

*6 large egg yolks,
at room temperature*

•

⅓ cup (75 g)
*Vanilla Sugar (page 22),
divided*

PREHEAT THE OVEN TO 300°F (150°C)

FOUR SHALLOW ¾-CUP (175 ML) RAMEKINS, SHALLOW OVENPROOF DISHES OR MASON JARS (SEE TIPS)

ROASTING PAN

PROPANE OR BUTANE TORCH (OPTIONAL)

1 In a medium bowl, whisk together the cream, egg yolks and ¼ cup (55 g) vanilla sugar until well combined.

2 Divide the mixture evenly among the ramekins. Place the ramekins in a roasting pan. Pour hot water into the pan until it comes about halfway up the sides of the ramekins.

3 Bake on the middle rack of the preheated oven until the custard barely moves when gently shaken or a knife inserted in the center comes out clean, about 45 to 60 minutes.

4 Using tongs, remove the ramekins from the pan and let cool on a wire rack to room temperature, about 45 to 60 minutes. Cover and refrigerate for at least 6 hours or up to 4 days.

5 Just before serving, blot any excess moisture from the tops of the custards. Sprinkle the remaining vanilla sugar evenly over the custards, making sure the tops are completely covered. Turn each ramekin upside down and tap gently to remove excess sugar, then turn it upright. Light the torch and, holding the flame 2 to 3 inches (5 to 7.5 cm) from the surface, caramelize the sugar until it is evenly melted and dark amber brown, moving constantly so the sugar doesn't burn. (Alternatively, preheat the broiler. Place the ramekins on a baking sheet on the top rack and broil until the sugar is caramelized, about 2 to 5 minutes. Check the sugar constantly and rotate the baking sheet as needed so that all the ramekins caramelize evenly.)

6 Let stand until the caramelized sugar has set, about 15 minutes.

TIPS

Shallow ramekins work best here, because the heat will be more
evenly distributed during baking, which will reduce the risk of overcooking.

Not sure what to do with the leftover egg whites? Try making Italian
Almond Cookies (page 33) or freeze them for later (see page 17 for details).

These two-bite lime cups deliver extra zing thanks to a gingersnap base. They're a simplified version of the classic Key lime pie, but this recipe uses standard limes. If you want to use tart and tiny Key limes instead, you'll need between 16 and 20.

GINGER-CRUSTED LIME TARTS

4 limes

•

8 gingersnap cookies, each about 2 inches (5 cm) in diameter

•

1 can (14 oz or 300 mL) full-fat sweetened condensed milk

PREHEAT THE OVEN TO 350°F (180°C)

12-CUP MUFFIN PAN, LINED WITH 8 LIGHTLY GREASED PAPER LINERS

1 Grate 1 tablespoon (15 mL) zest from the limes, plus a generous pinch (about $\frac{1}{8}$ teaspoon/0.5 mL). Squeeze enough of the limes to make $\frac{1}{3}$ cup (75 mL) juice (reserve any extra for another use).

2 Place a gingersnap cookie in the bottom of each paper liner.

3 In a medium bowl, combine the condensed milk, 1 tablespoon (15 mL) lime zest and the lime juice; whisk together until smooth.

4 Spoon the filling evenly over the gingersnaps. Sprinkle the remaining lime zest over top.

5 Bake on the middle rack of the preheated oven until the filling is just set and doesn't jiggle when gently shaken, about 8 to 10 minutes (it should not begin to brown).

6 Place the pan on a wire rack and let cool to room temperature. Cover and refrigerate for at least 4 hours or up to 3 days. Enjoy cold or at room temperature.

TIPS

Any leftover lime zest and juice can be frozen for later use; see page 16 for details.

These tarts can be stored in an airtight container in the freezer for up to 6 months. Defrost in the refrigerator overnight or for 30 minutes on the counter at room temperature before eating.

Tradition says this casual English dessert originated at Eton College and is served at cricket matches. I say it's a brilliant way to turn broken meringues into a showstopper.

STRAWBERRY ETON MESS

3 cups (420 g)
sliced strawberries,
thawed if frozen, divided

•

2 cups (500 mL)
cold heavy or whipping
(35%) cream

•

1 package
(3½ oz/100 g;
8 nests) store-bought
meringue nests

BLENDER

ELECTRIC MIXER

1 Place half the strawberries in a blender; blend on high speed until smooth. Transfer to a medium bowl, add the remaining strawberries and let stand for 10 minutes.

2 In a large bowl, using an electric mixer on high speed, whip the cold cream until stiff peaks form.

3 Crumble 7 of the meringues over the whipped cream and gently fold into the cream.

4 In a small bowl, crumble the remaining meringue. Set aside.

5 Set aside ½ cup (125 mL) of the strawberry mixture. Gently fold the remaining strawberry mixture into the whipped cream mixture.

6 Spoon the whipped cream mixture into dessert bowls, dividing evenly. Top with the reserved strawberry mixture and sprinkle with the reserved meringue crumbs. Serve immediately.

TIPS

You can substitute blueberries, raspberries or a combination of both for some or all of the strawberries.

Got leftover homemade meringues (page 46)? Three small meringues are about equivalent to one store-bought nest. This recipe can easily be scaled down to accommodate just a few broken cookies.

Leftover Eton mess can be refrigerated in an airtight container for up to 2 days.

Eggnog is the fruitcake of holiday beverages. Some people love it, some people loathe it. Regardless of where your family members fall on the eggnog spectrum, this easy-to-make bread pudding will please them all, and it tastes great for breakfast or dessert. Even if you only like eggnog with rum, I've got you covered. Drizzle or drench this with Buttered Rum Sauce (page 210) and I promise not to look at the clock while you do.

EGGNOG BREAD PUDDING

6 cups (250 g) cubed cinnamon raisin bread (1-inch/2.5 cm cubes), about 6 to 9 slices (see Tips)

•

2 cups (500 mL) full-fat eggnog

•

4 large eggs

8-INCH (20 CM) SQUARE GLASS BAKING DISH, BUTTERED

1 Place the bread cubes in the prepared dish.

2 In a large bowl, whisk together the eggnog and eggs until smooth. Pour over the bread cubes. Stir gently to ensure that all the bread is coated. Cover and refrigerate for at least 1 hour or up to 1 day.

3 Preheat the oven to 375°F (190°C).

4 Bake on the middle rack of the preheated oven until puffed and golden brown and the center is set, about 35 to 45 minutes. Let stand for 15 minutes. Serve warm.

TIPS

Day-old bread works best for this recipe. If your bread is really fresh, cube it and spread in a single layer on a baking sheet. Bake in an oven preheated to 250°F (120°C) for 15 minutes, stirring occasionally. Let cool completely.

Leftover bread pudding can be covered and refrigerated for up to 5 days. Enjoy it cold or reheat gently in a microwave-safe bowl, using the microwave on High in 30-second intervals and breaking it apart in between, until warmed through.

CANDYLAND

This variation on caramel corn is light and crunchy. If you like your popcorn loaded, you can double the coating and increase the baking time to 45 minutes. But I'm pretty confident this version will do, since the lighter the coating, the more you can eat.

MAPLE POPCORN

6 cups (1.5 L)
popped popcorn
(see Tips)

•

1/2 cup (125 mL)
pure maple syrup

•

1/4 cup (60 g)
salted butter

PREHEAT THE OVEN TO 275°F (135°C)

CANDY/DEEP-FRY THERMOMETER (OPTIONAL)

RIMMED BAKING SHEET, LINED WITH PARCHMENT PAPER

1 Place the popcorn in a very large heatproof bowl, allowing plenty of room to toss when coating. (If you don't have one large enough, divide the popcorn between two bowls.)

2 In a medium saucepan, combine the maple syrup, butter and a pinch of salt. Bring to a boil over medium heat, stirring constantly. Continue boiling, without stirring, until a candy/deep-fry thermometer reads 260°F (125°C) or a drop in a glass of ice water forms a ball that holds its shape but is still soft when pressed with your fingers.

3 Drizzle the hot syrup over the popcorn, stirring constantly to coat the popcorn evenly. Spread the popcorn on the prepared baking sheet.

4 Bake on the middle rack of the preheated oven until the popcorn is crispy, about 30 minutes, stirring after 15 minutes.

5 Let cool slightly on the baking sheet before breaking apart the popcorn, about 15 minutes. Eat warm or let cool completely.

TIPS

For 6 cups (1.5 L) popped popcorn, start with about 1/4 cup (60 mL) kernels.

Leftover popcorn can be stored in an airtight container at room temperature for up to 2 weeks.

When I was growing up, Black Forest cake was the ultimate birthday cake — I loved the combination of dark chocolate and cherries. This fudge delivers the classic flavors without the fuss of constructing a layer cake. The hardest part is waiting for it to cool.

BLACK FOREST FUDGE

2 cups (380 g)
semisweet chocolate
chips

•

1 can (14 oz or 300 mL)
full-fat sweetened
condensed milk

•

1 cup (160 g) dried
cherries, divided

8-INCH (20 CM) SQUARE BAKING PAN, LINED WITH
PARCHMENT PAPER

1 In a large microwave-safe bowl, combine the chocolate chips and condensed milk. Heat in the microwave on High in 30-second intervals, stirring in between, until the chips have melted. (Alternatively, heat in a medium saucepan over low heat, stirring constantly, until the chips have melted.) Stir in ²/₃ cup (110 g) dried cherries.

2 Pour into the prepared pan, spreading the mixture flat. Sprinkle the remaining cherries on top, pressing lightly to adhere them to the surface.

3 Refrigerate until firm, about 1 hour, or overnight. Cut into squares.

TIP

Store the fudge in an airtight container at room temperature for up to 2 weeks.

These are like Turtles chocolates, only with salted pretzels instead of pecans. They snap when you bite them, so the puns just write themselves. If you're feeling ambitious, try making them with your own homemade Chewy Salted Caramels (page 177); otherwise, opt for your favorite brand of soft caramel.

PRETZEL SNAPS

24 bite-sized waffle pretzels (see Tips)

•

12 soft caramel cubes, cut in half

•

8 ounces (225 g) chopped bittersweet (dark) chocolate

TWO 10-INCH (25 CM) SQUARE SHEETS OF PARCHMENT PAPER

1 Place one sheet of parchment paper on a microwave-safe plate. Arrange half the pretzels on the paper and place a caramel half in the center of each pretzel. Microwave on High in 15-second intervals until the caramel is soft but not melted (you want it to sink into the pretzel holes but not pool on the plate). Transfer the parchment to a wire rack to cool slightly.

2 Repeat with the second sheet of parchment and the remaining pretzels and caramels.

3 Remove the pretzels from the parchment paper and place directly on the wire rack. Place one of the used sheets of parchment under the rack to catch any drips.

4 In a medium microwave-safe bowl, microwave the chocolate on High in 30-second intervals, stirring in between, until three-quarters of it has melted. Stir gently until all the chocolate has melted. (Alternatively, melt it on the stove; see page 15 for details.)

5 Spoon the melted chocolate evenly over the caramel pretzels (it's okay to leave some pretzel and caramel showing). Refrigerate the snaps for about 10 minutes to set.

TIPS

If you can't find bite-sized waffle pretzels, use mini twisted pretzels instead.

Store the snaps in an airtight container at room temperature for up to 2 weeks.

When I was growing up, my grandfather would arrive each Christmas with a big unwrapped cardboard box — no bow, no tag and no fanfare. Inside was a treasure trove of sweets, including cans of pop, hard candies and chocolate bars. Somewhere among all those goodies hid a single lump of gold: sponge toffee. It was the only time of year that Mom would allow this sticky, filling-yanking treat into the house. Today I can make it in minutes, any time I want. Despite the temptation, I save this recipe for special occasions and think of my grandfather with every bite.

SPONGE TOFFEE

2 cups (440 g) granulated sugar

•

1/2 cup (125 mL) corn syrup

•

4 teaspoons (20 mL) baking soda, sifted

LARGE SAUCEPAN, AT LEAST 4 INCHES (10 CM) DEEP

13- BY 9-INCH (33 BY 23 CM) METAL BAKING PAN, LINED WITH LIGHTLY GREASED PARCHMENT PAPER (SEE PAGE 13)

1 In a large, deep saucepan over medium heat, heat the sugar, corn syrup and 1/2 cup (125 mL) water, stirring occasionally, until it starts to boil. Increase the heat to medium-high and maintain a full boil (bubbles should cover the entire surface), without stirring, until the syrup turns deep amber and a small amount dropped into cold water forms hard threads, about 8 to 12 minutes. (If you have a candy thermometer, you're looking for 300°F/150°C.) As it cooks, if the syrup is dark in some areas and light in others, gently tilt the pan (and rotate it if you have a hot spot) to swirl it without stirring.

2 Stir in the baking soda, being careful not to splash yourself, as it will foam up.

3 Working quickly, pour the mixture into the prepared baking pan. Place the pan on a wire rack and let the toffee cool completely, about 1 to 2 hours. Remove cooled toffee from the pan using the parchment paper overhang, then break it apart.

TIPS

When you grease the parchment, also consider greasing the measuring cup for the corn syrup. That will help it slide out easily without scraping.

Sugar burns very quickly; do not turn your back on the boiling sugar syrup for even a moment. However, if even your best efforts result in slightly burnt sugar, don't despair: some people actually find that flavor more appealing!

Moisture will quickly turn your crispy toffee into a sticky mess. If it's humid, eat it quickly. If it's not, store it in an airtight container at room temperature for up to 1 week. Never refrigerate sponge toffee.

There's something comforting about soft caramels that hard candies, no matter how colorful, just can't deliver. Is it the ritual of untwisting the wrapper? Is it the way the caramel yields when bitten into? Or is it the buttery sweetness that melts as you chew? I'm not 100 percent sure. I'd better go do more research.

CHEWY SALTED CARAMELS

2 cups (440 g) granulated sugar

•

⅔ cup (150 mL) heavy or whipping (35%) cream

•

½ cup (115 g) salted butter, cut into cubes

LARGE, HEAVY-BOTTOMED SAUCEPAN

CANDY/DEEP-FRY THERMOMETER (OPTIONAL)

8-INCH (20 CM) SQUARE BAKING PAN, LINED WITH PARCHMENT PAPER

SIXTY-FOUR 4-INCH (10 CM) SQUARES OF PARCHMENT PAPER

1 In a large, heavy-bottomed saucepan, heat the sugar over medium heat until it's beginning to melt and the edges are browning. Using a whisk, pull the brown bits into the center to avoid burning. If the sugar looks lumpy or grainy, lower the heat and keep stirring gently; the lumps should melt. Continue cooking until the sugar turns amber and is just beginning to smoke.

2 Remove from the heat and carefully whisk in the cream (be careful, as it will bubble up and splatter).

3 Return to medium heat and cook, stirring constantly, until a candy/deep-fry thermometer reads 250°F (120°C) or a drop in a glass of ice water forms a ball that holds its shape but is still very soft when pressed with your fingers.

4 Remove from the heat. Stir in the butter and a generous pinch of salt.

5 Pour into the prepared pan. Let stand until firm enough to cut, at least 4 hours, or overnight.

6 Turn out the caramel onto a cutting board and peel off the paper. Using a sharp knife, cut it into 1-inch (2.5 cm) squares. Wrap each piece in a parchment paper square and twist the ends to seal. Store at room temperature for up to 2 weeks.

TIP

If you like extra-salty salted caramels, sprinkle them with a pinch of sea salt just before eating. Do not sprinkle the caramels ahead of time, because the salt will cause them to melt.

This is a homemade version of the candy many of us snacked on as kids. Be warned: these are very sticky, so don't give them to anyone with dentures or loose fillings. Instead, give them to me.

SESAME SNAPS

1 cup (220 g) granulated sugar

•

1 cup (250 mL) honey

•

1 cup (125 g) toasted sesame seeds (see Tips)

MEDIUM, HEAVY-BOTTOMED SAUCEPAN

CANDY/DEEP-FRY THERMOMETER (OPTIONAL)

RIMMED BAKING SHEET, LINED WITH A GREASED DOUBLE LAYER OF FOIL OR A SILICONE MAT

1 In a medium, heavy-bottomed saucepan, combine the sugar and honey. Bring to a boil over medium heat, stirring occasionally. Boil, without stirring, until the mixture is dark amber and a candy/deep-fry thermometer reads 300°F (155°C) or a small drop in very cold water separates into strands that break if you try to bend them, about 15 to 20 minutes.

2 Quickly stir in the sesame seeds and a generous pinch of salt. Immediately pour onto the prepared baking sheet, spreading the mixture with a greased spatula to about 1/8 inch (3 mm) thick. Place the pan on a wire rack and let stand for 10 minutes.

3 Using a greased knife, score the mixture into 32 squares. (If you want smaller snaps, score each square in half diagonally). If the score marks melt back into the mixture, the mixture hasn't set enough. Wait longer and try scoring again.

4 Let the snaps cool completely, about 2 hours, then break along the score lines.

TIPS

Toasting sesame seeds brings out their nutty flavor. To toast sesame seeds, heat a dry small skillet over medium heat. Add the seeds and stir continuously until they turn pale golden brown, about 3 to 5 minutes. Immediately remove from the heat and transfer to a plate or bowl.

Store the snaps in an airtight container at room temperature for up to 1 week.

I started making nut brittle for a cooking class. Having practiced the recipe a few times, I had amassed a stockpile of it, which I took to a holiday party. When I saw all the flashy chocolate truffles and colorful cookies, I figured my humble brown-on-brown brittle would go unnoticed. I was wrong — it was devoured. "I haven't had this in years!" everyone said with their mouth full. Seems that nostalgia, no matter how plain, always has a place at the table.

MIXED NUT BRITTLE

2 cups (440 g) granulated sugar

•

3 cups (450 g) salted roasted mixed nuts

•

1 teaspoon (5 mL) flaky sea salt

RIMMED BAKING SHEET, LINED WITH PARCHMENT PAPER

1 In a large saucepan over medium heat, combine the sugar and ¾ cup (175 mL) water. Heat, occasionally stirring gently and being careful not to splash the sides, until the sugar dissolves. Increase the heat to medium-high and bring to a boil, without stirring. (If the sugar has splashed the sides of the saucepan, brush away the splatters with a wet pastry brush to prevent their burning.) Continue boiling, without stirring, until the sugar turns a deep amber, about 12 to 20 minutes. Immediately remove it from the heat and quickly stir in the nuts.

2 Pour the hot brittle over the prepared baking sheet and sprinkle with flaky salt. Place the pan on a wire rack and let the brittle cool completely, about 2 hours.

3 Remove the brittle from the pan using the parchment liner and place it on a cutting board. Break it into pieces using a rolling pin or mallet.

TIPS

If you don't have salted roasted nuts on hand, toast nuts in an oven preheated to 350°F (180°C) for 7 to 10 minutes or until fragrant. Add a generous pinch of salt to the brittle when you add the nuts.

Don't toss the brittle crumbs. Save them to sprinkle on ice cream.

For a scrub-free cleanup, fill the saucepan with enough water to cover any remaining sugar, pop the spoon into the pot, and heat on the stovetop until the water is very hot (almost boiling). The sugar will dissolve.

Store the brittle in an airtight container at room temperature for up to 2 weeks.

My grandmother used to make candied peel at Christmas. I would sneak a piece every time I went past the candy bowl, stopping only when I had reached the stomachache stage of childhood gluttony. Despite my soft spot for this treat, making it seemed like too much work. All the vintage recipes call for peeling the citrus, triple batches of boiling and days of drying. Thanks to a vegetable peeler, I've managed to streamline the process. Now I just have to exercise self-restraint.

CHOCOLATE-DIPPED CANDIED ORANGE PEEL

3 navel oranges

•

1 cup (220 g) granulated sugar, plus ¼ cup (55 g) for rolling

•

4 ounces (115 g) bittersweet (dark) chocolate, chopped

BAKING SHEET, LINED WITH PARCHMENT PAPER

1 Using a vegetable peeler, peel the oranges, making sure you remove only the colorful outer layer and leave the bitter white pith (reserve the oranges for another use). Cut each piece of peel into strips ¼ inch (0.5 cm) wide; the lengths will vary.

2 Fill a medium saucepan halfway with water and bring to a boil over high heat. Add the peels and simmer for 5 minutes to remove bitterness. Drain, discarding the water.

3 In the same saucepan over medium-high heat, bring the sugar and 1 cup (250 mL) water to a boil. Immediately reduce the heat to medium-low and add the peels; simmer, uncovered and without stirring, until the peels are translucent and the syrup has thickened, about 20 to 25 minutes.

4 Remove the saucepan from the heat and let the peels cool in the syrup. Using a slotted spoon or fork, remove the strips of peel from the syrup and place on a wire rack set over paper towels. Leave until tacky, about 1 hour.

5 Place ¼ cup (55 g) sugar on a plate. Roll the strips of peel in the sugar to coat them, then return to the rack to dry, about 4 hours.

6 In a small microwave-safe bowl, microwave the chocolate on High in 30-second intervals, stirring in between, until three-quarters of it is melted. Stir gently until all the chocolate has melted. (Alternatively, melt it on the stove; see page 15.)

7 Dip one end of each sugared peel in the chocolate. Place on the prepared baking sheet and let stand until the chocolate has hardened. Store in an airtight container with parchment paper between the layers. The candied peel will keep at room temperature for up to 2 weeks.

COLD THINGS

No ice-cream maker? No problem. Sweetened condensed milk (not evaporated milk) is the key ingredient in this recipe. Lightened with whipped cream, this ice cream needs no churning yet is decadent enough to be embraced by every food guru from Martha to Nigella.

VANILLA ICE CREAM

1 can (14 oz or 300 mL) full-fat sweetened condensed milk

•

2 teaspoons (10 mL) vanilla extract

•

2 cups (500 mL) cold heavy or whipping (35%) cream

ELECTRIC MIXER

FREEZER-SAFE 1-QUART (1 L) CONTAINER OR 9- BY 5-INCH (23 BY 12.5 CM) LOAF PAN, LINED WITH PLASTIC WRAP OR PARCHMENT PAPER

1 In a large bowl, combine the condensed milk, vanilla and a pinch of salt.

2 In a separate large bowl, using an electric mixer on high speed, whip the cold cream until stiff peaks form.

3 Fold about 1/2 cup (125 mL) whipped cream into the condensed milk mixture. Gently fold in the remaining whipped cream.

4 Spoon the mixture into the prepared container. Place a piece of plastic wrap directly on the surface to prevent ice from forming. Freeze until firm, at least 6 hours, or overnight.

5 Let stand on the counter for 15 minutes to soften before serving.

TIP

The ice cream can keep for up to 1 month, but it gets harder the longer it's frozen. For the best results, consume it within 2 weeks.

I used to make salted caramel ice cream the old-fashioned way, by caramelizing sugar, cooking an egg-rich custard, chilling, then churning, then chilling again. Then I got smart. This no-churn version delivers the same flavor and creamy texture but with far less work. As an added bonus, there are fewer dishes to clean up.

SALTED CARAMEL ICE CREAM

1 cup (250 mL)
dulce de leche

•

1/2 teaspoon (2 mL)
flaky sea salt (see Tips),
approx.

•

2 cups (500 mL)
cold heavy or whipping
(35%) cream

ELECTRIC MIXER

FREEZER-SAFE 1-QUART (1 L) CONTAINER OR 9- BY 5-INCH (23 BY 12.5 CM) LOAF PAN, LINED WITH PLASTIC WRAP OR PARCHMENT PAPER

1 In a large bowl, combine the dulce de leche and salt.

2 In a separate large bowl, using an electric mixer on high speed, beat the cold cream until stiff peaks form.

3 Stir one-third of the whipped cream into the dulce de leche mixture until just combined. Gently fold in the remaining whipped cream.

4 Spoon into the prepared container. Place a piece of plastic wrap directly on the surface to prevent ice from forming. Freeze until firm, at least 6 hours, or overnight.

5 Serve with an additional bit of flaky sea salt sprinkled over top, if desired.

TIPS

If you don't have flaky sea salt, use 1/8 teaspoon (0.5 mL) table salt instead.

Because of its high sugar content, this ice cream will remain very soft. Return any uneaten ice cream to the freezer immediately.

Because of its soft texture, this ice cream will keep in the freezer for up to 1 month, which is a bit longer than some of the other ice-cream recipes in this chapter.

When my grandmother served us rainbow sherbet, I would mix the lime, orange and raspberry flavors together, creating a khaki-colored mess. My sister, who methodically ate one flavor at a time, complained loudly that I was ruining my dessert and her appetite. My grandmother calmly defended my dubious choice: "It's her sherbet. She can do what she wants." Vindicated! Today, being slightly more mature and arguably less defiant, I make peach sherbet — monochromatic, peacekeeping, summer-kissed peach sherbet. Stir it if you like. I won't mind.

PEACH SHERBET

1 cup (250 mL)
table (18%) cream

•

4 cups (560 g)
frozen sliced peaches

•

²/₃ cup (150 g)
Vanilla Sugar (page 22)

BLENDER

4 ICE-CUBE TRAYS

FREEZER-SAFE 1-QUART (1 L) CONTAINER OR 9- BY 5-INCH (23 BY 12.5 CM) LOAF PAN, LINED WITH PLASTIC WRAP OR PARCHMENT PAPER

1 In a blender, combine the cream, peaches and sugar. Blend on high speed, stopping the motor to scrape down the sides of the container as necessary, until smooth.

2 Pour the peach mixture into the ice-cube trays, cover and freeze until firm, at least 2 hours, or overnight.

3 Place the frozen peach cubes in the blender; blend on high speed until smooth and creamy (like melting soft-serve ice cream).

4 Pour the mixture into the prepared container. Place a piece of plastic wrap directly on the surface to prevent ice from forming. Freeze until firm, at least 4 hours, or overnight. When serving, return any uneaten sherbet to the freezer immediately.

TIPS

If you don't have enough ice-cube trays, pour the sherbet mixture into a 13- by 9-inch (33 by 23 cm) metal baking pan, lined with plastic wrap or parchment paper, and freeze. Once frozen, cut it into pieces with a sharp knife and blend as directed.

For a Peach Melba variation, drizzle Raspberry Sauce (page 211) over your bowl of sherbet.

The sherbet will keep in the freezer for up to 3 months.

It doesn't feel like summer until the strawberries arrive. This simple recipe can be made with fresh or frozen strawberries, so you can enjoy a taste of summer no matter what the calendar says.

STRAWBERRY ICE CREAM

3 cups (420 g) sliced strawberries, thawed if frozen

•

½ cup (110 g) granulated sugar

•

1 cup (250 mL) cold heavy or whipping (35%) cream

ELECTRIC MIXER

FREEZER-SAFE 1-QUART (1 L) CONTAINER OR 9- BY 5-INCH (23 BY 12.5 CM) LOAF PAN, LINED WITH PLASTIC WRAP OR PARCHMENT PAPER

1 In a large bowl, combine the strawberries and sugar; toss to coat. Set aside for at least 1 hour or cover and refrigerate for up to 24 hours.

2 Using a fork, crush the strawberries until smooth, with just a few lumps remaining. (Alternatively, transfer the strawberries and juices from the bowl to a food processor; pulse in 3-second intervals until mostly smooth.)

3 In a medium bowl, using an electric mixer on high speed, whip the cold cream until stiff peaks form. Fold the strawberry mixture into the cream, leaving some swirls.

4 Pour the ice-cream mixture into the prepared container. Place a piece of plastic wrap directly on the surface to prevent ice from forming. Freeze until firm, about 6 hours, or overnight.

5 Let stand on the counter for 15 minutes to soften before serving.

TIPS

Cream whips best when it's very cold. If your kitchen is warm, chill the bowl and mixer beaters for 10 minutes before whipping the cream.

The ice cream can keep for up to 1 month, but it gets harder the longer it's frozen. For the best results, consume it within 2 weeks.

Mangos are magical. While most sorbets need a bit of alcohol to keep them from becoming granular and icy, mangos keep things creamy and smooth — no booze required. Of course, if you want to add a splash for luck, I won't stop you.

MANGO SORBET

4 cups (600 g) frozen mango chunks

•

3 tablespoons (45 mL) freshly squeezed lime juice

•

2 tablespoons (30 mL) liquid honey

BLENDER OR FOOD PROCESSOR

FREEZER-SAFE 1-QUART (1 L) CONTAINER OR 9- BY 5-INCH (23 BY 12.5 CM) LOAF PAN, LINED WITH PLASTIC WRAP OR PARCHMENT PAPER

1 Let the frozen mango soften on the counter for 30 minutes. (Alternatively, thaw it slightly in a large microwave-safe bowl in the microwave on Defrost for 5 minutes.) The mango chunks should be cold but softened enough that you can pierce them easily with a sharp knife.

2 Place the lime juice, honey and mango in a blender or food processor. Blend on high speed until smooth, about 3 to 4 minutes, stopping the motor as needed to scrape down the sides of the container.

3 Pour the mixture into the prepared container. Place a piece of plastic wrap directly on the surface to prevent ice from forming. Freeze until firm, at least 4 hours, or overnight. When serving, return any uneaten sorbet to the freezer immediately.

TIPS

Because mangos make a creamy base, you can easily experiment with fruit combinations and still maintain a smooth texture. Try adding strawberries, pineapple or peaches. Just be sure that at least 2 cups (300 g) of the fruit is mango.

The sorbet will keep for up to 3 months. If it has been frozen for an extended time, let it stand at room temperature for 10 minutes before scooping.

I grew up eating granular homemade Kool-Aid ice pops, which cooled us down but didn't exactly excite us. Every once in a while a box of orange Creamsicles would make its way into our freezer. I adored how their icy orange coating gave way to a creamy vanilla interior. Even without the orange shell, the taste of these smooth-textured ice pops still takes me back to my childhood. They're like a ray of sunshine on a stick.

ORANGE ICE POPS

1 cup (250 mL)
frozen orange juice
concentrate, thawed

•

1 cup (250 mL)
heavy or whipping
(35%) cream

•

¼ cup (55 g)
Vanilla Sugar (page 22)

4 TO 6 ICE-POP MOLDS

1 In a medium bowl, whisk together the orange juice concentrate, cream and sugar until combined.

2 Pour the mixture into ice-pop molds and freeze until solid, at least 6 hours, or overnight.

3 To unmold the ice pops, fill a deep bowl with hot water. Dip a mold into the water, being careful to stop before the water reaches the top edge. Submerge in 15-second intervals until the pop releases from the mold.

TIPS

Stir any leftover orange juice concentrate into plain yogurt and top with granola, or add it to a smoothie.

The ice pops will keep in the freezer for up to 2 months.

When I was a broke student touring Greece, the youth hostels were closed during the day and I was forced to seek refuge from the heat on covered restaurant patios. Not wanting to drink alcohol so early in the day, and having little money, I downed endless glasses of refreshing, inexpensive iced coffee. These frosty, cooling pops remind me of those carefree days spent under cloudless skies.

ICED COFFEE FROZEN POPS

2 cups (500 mL) hot, strong brewed coffee

•

¹/₂ cup (110 g) Vanilla Sugar (page 22)

•

1 cup (250 mL) heavy or whipping (35%) cream

6 TO 9 ICE-POP MOLDS

1 In a medium bowl, combine the hot coffee and sugar; stir constantly until the sugar dissolves. Let the mixture cool to room temperature.

2 Stir the cream into the coffee mixture. Pour into ice-pop molds and freeze until solid, at least 6 hours, or overnight.

3 To unmold the ice pops, fill a deep bowl with hot water. Dip a mold into the water, being careful to stop before the water reaches the top edge. Submerge in 15-second intervals until the pop releases from the mold.

TIPS

For variety, make this with your favorite flavored coffee.

If you like your coffee less sweet, reduce the Vanilla Sugar to ¹/₄ cup (55 g).

The ice pops will keep in the freezer for up to 2 months.

I refuse to reveal whether the inspiration for these came from caring about my lactose-free friends or my love of coconut. Regardless, these ice pops deliver full-on coconut flavor without a drop of dairy. Like extra coconut? Roll your ice pop in some before you eat. Like yours plain? Dive straight in. Everybody wins!

DAIRY-FREE COCONUT ICE POPS

1 can (12.2 oz/360 mL) full-fat evaporated coconut milk

•

1 can (7.4 oz/220 mL) full-fat sweetened condensed coconut milk

•

½ cup (50 g) toasted unsweetened shredded coconut, plus ½ cup (50 g) for optional rolling (see Tips)

6 TO 9 ICE-POP MOLDS

1 In a large bowl, combine the evaporated coconut milk and the condensed coconut milk. Stir in ½ cup (50 g) toasted coconut.

2 Pour the mixture into ice-pop molds and freeze overnight.

3 To unmold the ice pops, fill a deep bowl with hot water. Dip a mold into the water, being careful to stop before the water reaches the top edge. Submerge in 15-second intervals until the pop releases from the mold. Eat the ice pops as is or roll in an additional ½ cup (50 g) coconut before serving, if desired.

TIPS

Sweetened condensed coconut milk and evaporated coconut milk can be found in the health food section of many well-stocked grocery stores, at most health food stores and online.

To toast the coconut, heat a dry medium skillet over medium heat. Add the shredded coconut and stir continuously until it turns pale golden brown, about 2 to 5 minutes. Remove from the heat immediately and transfer to a plate or bowl.

The ice pops will keep in the freezer for up to 2 months.

It's true that alcohol makes ice cream and sorbets less granular. But it's also my excuse to open a bottle of sparkling wine and get creative. These refreshing pops, featuring tangy grapefruit, make a welcome addition to barbecue dinners and patio brunches. Can they be enjoyed for breakfast? If you're on vacation, why not?

SPARKLING GRAPEFRUIT POPS

¾ cup (165 g) granulated sugar

•

1 cup (250 mL) Champagne-style sparkling white wine, divided

•

2 cups (500 mL) ruby red grapefruit juice

6 TO 9 ICE-POP MOLDS

1 In a medium saucepan over medium-high heat, heat the sugar and ½ cup (125 mL) wine, stirring occasionally, until the sugar is dissolved, about 2 minutes. Remove from the heat. Stir in the remaining wine and the grapefruit juice.

2 Pour the mixture into ice-pop molds and freeze until solid, at least 6 hours, or overnight.

3 To unmold the ice pops, fill a deep bowl with hot water. Dip a mold into the water, being careful to stop before the water reaches the top edge. Submerge in 15-second intervals until the pop releases from the mold.

TIPS

If you'd prefer a more "adult" version of these pops, you can easily serve this as a sorbet. Simply freeze the mixture from Step 1 in ice-cube trays instead of ice-pop molds. Transfer the frozen cubes to a blender and blend on high speed until smooth. Freeze in an airtight container until solid, about 6 hours.

The ice pops will keep in the freezer for up to 2 months.

Tart raspberries and sweet white chocolate come together in these colorful, fudgy ice pops. Take them to picnic potlucks or keep some in the freezer for a post-lawn-cutting reward — or as a just-because treat. For a fun variation, try coating the pops with Hard-Top Chocolate Sauce (page 208).

WHITE CHOCOLATE AND RASPBERRY ICE POPS

8 ounces (225 g)
white chocolate, chopped

•

1 cup (250 mL)
heavy or whipping
(35%) cream

•

¾ cup (105 g)
frozen raspberries,
thawed

ELECTRIC MIXER

4 TO 6 ICE-POP MOLDS

1 In a large microwave-safe bowl, combine the white chocolate and cream. Heat in the microwave in 30-second intervals, stirring in between, until the chocolate has melted. (Alternatively, melt it on the stove; see page 15 for details.) Cover and refrigerate until cold, about 30 minutes.

2 Using an electric mixer on high speed, beat the cooled mixture until soft peaks form, about 8 to 10 minutes.

3 In a small bowl, stir the thawed berries to break them up. Fold into the whipped chocolate mixture.

4 Spoon the mixture into ice-pop molds, tapping them on a hard surface to get out any air bubbles. Freeze until firm, at least 4 hours, or overnight.

5 To unmold the ice pops, fill a deep bowl with hot water. Dip a mold into the water, being careful to stop before the water reaches the top edge. Submerge in 15-second intervals until the pop releases from the mold.

TIPS

Try using milk chocolate or bittersweet (dark) chocolate for a taste variation.

The ice pops will keep in the freezer for up to 2 months.

SAUCES & TOPPINGS

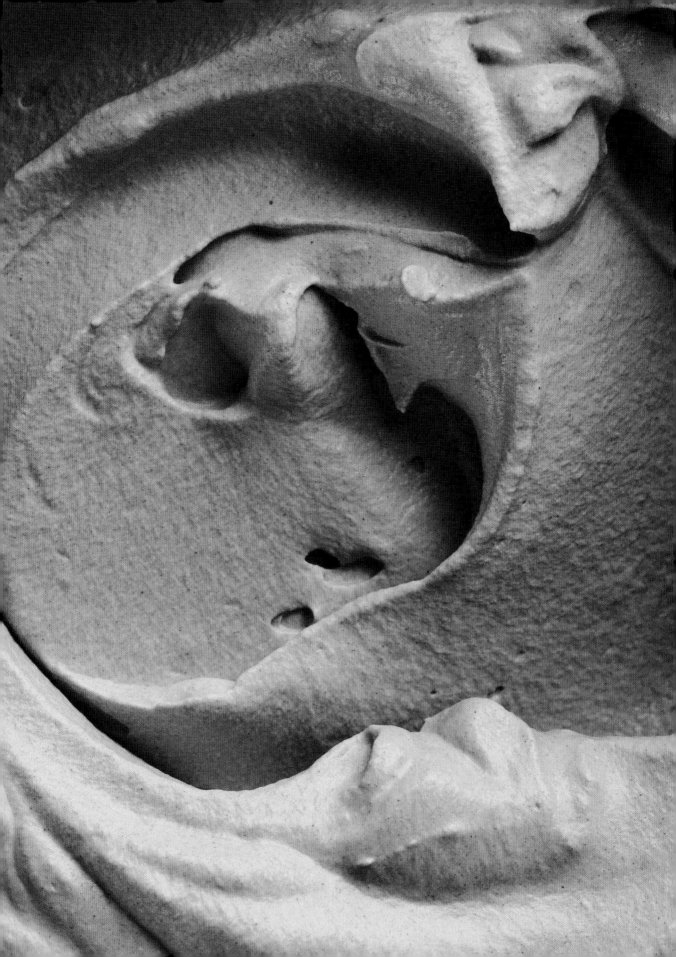

What's wrong with plain old whipped cream? Nothing. So why mess with success? Let's flip the question. What's wrong with chocolate whipped cream? Nothing, nothing at all. When you feel like a change of pace, give this a try and see if you agree. Add a spoonful to Peach Cobbler (page 149), Raspberry Ice-Cream Muffins (page 85) or Maple Panna Cotta Pots (page 157).

CHOCOLATE WHIPPED CREAM

2 cups (500 mL)
cold heavy or whipping
(35%) cream

•

$^1/_4$ cup (25 g)
unsweetened cocoa
powder

•

$^1/_2$ cup (65 g)
confectioners'
(icing) sugar

ELECTRIC MIXER

1 In a large bowl, using an electric mixer on low speed, beat together the cold cream, cocoa powder and confectioners' sugar until well combined. Increase the speed to high and beat until stiff peaks form. Use immediately or cover and refrigerate for up to 3 days.

TIPS

If your confectioners' sugar or cocoa powder is lumpy, sift them together through a fine-mesh sieve before adding them to the cream. A lump-free mixture will ensure a more even whip.

Whipping cream can be messy. If you're using an electric hand mixer, you can place the bowl in your sink to catch any splatter. Alternatively, drape a tea towel over the bowl and mixer and keep it in place until the cream begins to thicken.

When I was growing up, whipped cream was always sweetened with a hint of vanilla. I had no idea there was any other way to make it. Turns out Mom had been making Chantilly cream all those years. Instead of using granulated sugar, this version uses confectioners' sugar, which adds to its stability, making it an ideal make-ahead option.

CHANTILLY CREAM

2 cups (500 mL) cold heavy or whipping (35%) cream

•

¼ cup (35 g) confectioners' (icing) sugar

•

1 teaspoon (5 mL) vanilla extract

ELECTRIC MIXER

1 In a large bowl, using an electric mixer on high speed, beat together the cold cream, confectioners' sugar and vanilla until stiff peaks form. Use immediately or cover and store in the refrigerator for up to 3 days.

TIP

Cream whips best when cold. If your kitchen is warm, pop the cream into the freezer and the bowl and beaters into the refrigerator for 10 minutes before you whip.

When my sisters and I came in from the cold after skating, Mom warmed us up with hot chocolate. She made the sauce herself, but I wanted mine from the bottle with the rabbit on it — the one all the other kids had. Once I realized Mom's sauce was so easy to make that we'd never run out, I stopped feeling hard done by and learned how to do it myself. Thanks to its 1:1:1 ratio, I had the recipe memorized in no time.

MOM'S DRIPPY CHOCOLATE SAUCE

1 cup (220 g)
granulated sugar

•

1 cup (95 g)
unsweetened cocoa
powder

•

Pinch fine sea salt

1 In a medium saucepan, combine the sugar, cocoa powder and 1 cup (250 mL) water. Add a pinch of sea salt. Bring to a boil over medium-high heat, stirring constantly. Immediately reduce the heat to medium-low and simmer, stirring constantly, for 3 minutes.

2 Remove from the heat and let cool. Serve warm or at room temperature.

TIPS

If you're making the sauce ahead or have any leftovers, transfer it to an airtight container. Let the warm sauce cool, uncovered, to room temperature, then place plastic wrap directly on the surface to prevent a skin from forming. The sauce will keep, covered, for up to 1 month.

To warm, remove the plastic wrap and transfer to a microwave-safe bowl. Microwave on High in 15-second intervals, stirring in between, until warm. (Alternatively, warm it in a small saucepan over medium-low heat, stirring occasionally.)

When I was a kid, one of the highlights of summer was a trip to the park and a vanilla soft-serve ice cream encased in a chocolate shell. The best part was cracking the coating, despite the fact that the chocolate had little taste. Nowadays I want both texture and taste. Thanks to the popularity of coconut oil, delicious homemade hard-shell chocolate sauce is minutes away, any time you want. And cracking the shell? That never gets old.

HARD-TOP CHOCOLATE SAUCE

8 ounces (225 g) 70% bittersweet (dark) chocolate, chopped

•

¾ cup (165 g) coconut oil (see Tips)

•

¼ cup (60 mL) corn syrup

1 In a medium microwave-safe bowl, combine the chocolate, coconut oil and corn syrup. Microwave on High in 15-second intervals, stirring in between, until the chocolate has melted. (Alternatively, heat it in a medium saucepan over medium heat, stirring occasionally, until the chocolate has melted.)

2 Add a generous pinch of salt and stir well to combine.

3 Pour the sauce onto ice cream. Within about 30 seconds, it will form a shell. You'll know it has hardened when the chocolate is no longer shiny and looks a bit dull.

TIPS

Virgin coconut oil will add more of a coconut flavor to the sauce. If you don't want a coconut taste, use refined coconut oil. As long as the coconut oil is solid at room temperature, it will do the trick. Do not use MCT (medium-chain triglyceride) coconut oil, which is liquid at room temperature.

For easy pouring, transfer the sauce to a squeeze bottle.

Store the sauce at room temperature (not in the refrigerator) in an airtight container for up to 1 month. If the sauce hardens, warm it slightly in a small microwave-safe bowl, microwaving on Medium in 15-second intervals until it loosens, or place the squeeze bottle in a bowl of hot water for 2 minutes.

Give this a cape and contact Marvel, because this sauce has superpowers. It can rescue dried-out cake with a single pour, transport frosty ice cream to another dimension and leap straight from the spoon into your mouth. Kapow! Try it on Eggnog Bread Pudding (page 165), Vanilla Ice Cream (page 184) or Peach Cobbler (page 149).

BUTTERED RUM SAUCE

1 cup (220 g)
granulated sugar

•

1/2 cup (115 g)
*salted butter,
cut into cubes*

•

1/2 cup (125 mL)
rum (see Tips)

1 In a medium saucepan, heat the sugar, butter and rum over medium-low heat, stirring occasionally, until the butter has melted, about 3 minutes. Add a generous pinch of salt, then increase the heat to medium-high and bring to a boil. Boil, stirring constantly, for 3 minutes.

2 Let cool for about 15 minutes. Serve warm.

TIPS

I like this made with dark rum, but white or amber works just as well.
Don't have rum? Try bourbon or Canadian whisky.

If you're making the sauce ahead or have any leftovers, transfer it to an airtight container. Let the warm sauce cool to room temperature, then place plastic wrap directly on the surface to prevent a skin from forming. The sauce will keep, covered, in the refrigerator for up to 2 weeks.

Don't worry if the sauce separates as it cools. To recombine, transfer it to a medium microwave-safe bowl and break up the solidified butter with a fork. Microwave on High in 15-second intervals, stirring in between, until warm. Alternatively, warm it in a small saucepan over medium heat, stirring occasionally.

I don't know why grocery store shelves aren't bursting with bottles of raspberry sauce. Sure, chocolate and caramel have proven themselves, but raspberry sauce continues to fly under the radar. This underappreciated ruby-red sauce delivers tang and plays so well with so many things it should be a standard pantry item. Try it on Banana Pancakes (page 87), Mandarin Muffins (page 86), Maple Panna Cotta Pots (page 157) or Vanilla Ice Cream (page 184). I could go on, but you get the idea.

RASPBERRY SAUCE

4 cups (560 g) frozen raspberries (see Tips)

•

⅓ cup (75 g) Citrus Sugar (page 21)

•

1 tablespoon (15 mL) vanilla extract

FINE-MESH SIEVE

1 In a medium saucepan over medium-high heat, bring the raspberries, citrus sugar and vanilla to a boil, stirring occasionally. Immediately reduce the heat to a simmer and cook, stirring occasionally, until the berries have broken down, about 5 minutes.

2 Place a fine-mesh sieve over a medium heatproof bowl. Pour the raspberry mixture into the sieve and, using a ladle or large spoon, press through the mesh, stopping occasionally to scrape sauce from the outside of the sieve. Discard the seeds.

3 Serve the sauce warm or at room temperature.

TIPS

Freezing breaks down the cell structure of berries, making them fall apart easily. If you are using fresh raspberries, you might have to add 2 to 4 tablespoons (30 to 60 mL) of water while they cook to help them break down.

The sauce will keep in the refrigerator for up to 4 days. Use it straight from the fridge or warm it in the microwave in 15-second intervals, stirring in between. (Alternatively, warm it in a small saucepan over medium-low heat, stirring occasionally.)

The title almost says it all. All that's missing is "Serendipitous," but that's too much of a mouthful. I created this sauce by mistake when I added too much cream to Caramelized White Chocolate Truffles (page 126). Never one to waste things, I turned the potential disaster into a sauce. The salt-kissed result goes well with ice cream, Pear and Almond Pies (page 104) or Peach Cobbler (page 149).

SALTED CARAMELIZED WHITE CHOCOLATE SAUCE

8 ounces (230 g) caramelized white chocolate (page 126, Step 1), chopped

•

1 cup (250 mL) heavy or whipping (35%) cream

•

Pinch fine sea salt (approx.)

1 Place the chopped white chocolate in a medium heatproof bowl. Set aside.

2 In a small saucepan over medium heat, heat the cream until bubbles form around the edges. Do not boil.

3 Remove from the heat and pour the hot cream over the chocolate. Let stand for 1 minute. Stir until smooth and combined. Add a pinch of fine sea salt. Taste and add more salt if needed. Serve warm or at room temperature.

TIPS

Store any leftover sauce in an airtight container in the refrigerator for up to 1 week.

To warm refrigerated sauce, transfer to a medium microwave-safe bowl. Microwave on High in 15-second intervals, stirring in between, until warm. (Alternatively, warm it in a small saucepan over medium-low heat, stirring occasionally.)

ACKNOWLEDGMENTS

Simplicity can be deceptive. Although these recipes use only three ingredients, it took a large and often unseen team to make this book happen. I send chocolate-covered kisses to my friends and family for their support. To my publishing team, I offer a more professional platter of cookies.

Thanks to the following people. The order is random. I put your names in a saucepan and drew to avoid being accused of playing favorites. A drum roll please, for:

Emily Richards, who got this whole three-ingredient ball rolling. I appreciate your faith in me.

My long-suffering husband, Andrew. You never complained as the manuscript crept from the kitchen to the dining area, to the living room, and threatened to break down your office door. Your patience, understanding and love kept me going long after the sugar crash. Next time you ask for shortbread, my response will not be "Again?!" but rather "How many?"

My sister Robin, who came, washed dishes, helped with setup, fetched ingredients, ran electrical cords and tested recipes, yet kept apologizing for not doing more. You get Chocolate Mousse for life.

My sister Allison, who did dishes, shared dinnerware, organized the pantry and found a creative solution for the ingredients that had invaded my life. Your enthusiastic response to the Lemon Ginger Parfaits gave me the boost I needed.

My mother: even though I broke one of your good Théodore Haviland Limoges fruit bowls (which I borrowed without asking) during a recipe test, you didn't disown me or give me a guilt trip. Instead you offered me more, any time I needed. You instilled my love of baking and continue to inspire me in the kitchen. I will make you Eton Mess any time you like.

My dad, who cleared yard waste and ran numerous errands while I baked (and cursed) through prime gardening season. For you, shortbread is no longer just for Christmas.

Meredith Dees, my editor, for making sure I didn't overcomplicate things when I was clearly overcomplicating things. Thanks for pointing me in the right direction when I was spinning in circles chasing squirrels.

Sue Sumeraj, my other editor, whose keen eyes, calm demeanor and consummate problem-solving kept the copy clean and me sane. This Sparkling Grapefruit Pop's for you.

Jennifer MacKenzie, for your keen eyes and finely tuned recipe sense. You make me look good. Take the last cookie. It's yours.

Bob Dees, whose perseverance and belief in this concept helped lead me to a big three-letter, three-ingredient *yes*. I was skeptical. You were wise.

The photography team whose creativity, talent and expertise brought these simple recipes to life. A big thanks to Lauren Miller, for bringing her photography skills and artistry to the overflowing table. To Rayna Schwartz, for her gorgeous props and unfailing smile. To Dara Sutin, for her attention to detail and mad food-styling skills.

Kevin Cockburn and the art department team, for bringing all the parts together in such a creative and inspiring way. Your vision for the book surpassed my wildest expectations.

INDEX